Praise for *A Life Beyond Reason*

"A poignant, powerfully written story of a radically mismanaged delivery at a major medical institution and the painful yet paradoxically luminous consequences of that catastrophe. Simultaneously a timely exploration of medical error, a moving disability memoir, and an elegy for the blithe spirit of a much-loved child, Gabbard's book will be must-reading not only for investigators of medical malpractice and theorists of disability but also for all who are awed by the intensity of parental devotion."

—SANDRA M. GILBERT, author of *Death's Door* and
coauthor of *The Madwoman in the Attic*

"The book is STUNNING. So eloquent and full of wisdom—and a certain tragicomic humor. I loved it. . . . The moral force of it is unquestionable—so real and overpowering but also unassuming in a lot of ways."

—TERRY CASTLE, author of *Masquerade and Civilization*

"If you have ever questioned the very foundation of your beliefs—you will want to read this book. If you have been misjudged, mistreated, misdiagnosed by the medical establishment—you will want to read this book. If you have been a caregiver for someone with disabilities—you will want to read this book. But most of all, if you have loved a child beyond measure, beyond compare—you *must* read this book. Chris Gabbard takes us along on his family's fourteen-year journey with August, his beautiful, beloved boy, who is also profoundly disabled. With clarity and grace, Gabbard describes the utterly indescribable, bringing it to life on the page. Early on in this haunting and moving book, Gabbard says, 'When intertwined, love and grief become as ferocious as desire.' As you turn the pages, you will come to understand precisely what he means."

—ANDREA LUNSFORD, author of *The Everyday Writer*

"It's hard to speak highly enough about the unforgettable book Chris Gabbard has written about his disabled son's life and times and the medical industrial complex that tested Gabbard's family beyond what any of us can imagine having to endure. This gorgeously eloquent memoir is excruciating in its impact, and is in the top most moving, troubling, and ultimately rewarding reading experiences I've ever had."

—ELIZABETH MCKENZIE, author of *The Portable Veblen*

"An extraordinary book, telling a story that needs to be told—and heard. It is a story of extreme caregiving, in Lisa Freitag's apt phrase; it is a story of medical malpractice and shredded social safety nets, an urgent message for our dark and austere political moment; it is also a story of enduring love, and the way that loving someone with a disability can change your world. Like Marianne Leone's *Knowing Jesse*, this bracingly unsentimental book is moving, illuminating, and deeply rewarding."

—MICHAEL BÉRUBÉ, author of *Life as Jamie Knows It*

"Gabbard describes with intelligence, knowledge, and feeling life with his profoundly disabled son, August. . . . A must-read for anyone interested in life's challenges and how complexly these are met and understood."

—LENNARD DAVIS, author of *My Sense of Silence*

"Gabbard deftly explores the fraught, overlapping territories of caregiving, parenting, disability, and medicine. Loving and unsentimental, the book—despite its weighty subject matter—has a kind of lightness, a hard-won calm. Gabbard is the scholar of his own joys and despairs, both passionate and dispassionate at once, and in this retrospective . . . he finds insight into himself, his family, and what it means to be human."

—GEORGE ESTREICH, author of *The Shape of the Eye*

"While investigating his son's traumatic birth, a father finds not only meaning but also joy in the profoundly disabled life that followed. This book movingly reconfigures questions of human worth and care, and it envisions a different role for medicine in the field of disability. Less elegy . . . than encomium, *A Life Beyond Reason* invites you to bask in its heartening warmth."

—RALPH JAMES SAVARESE, author of *Reasonable People*

"A compelling chronicle of one father's relentless quest to understand the circumstances around his son's 'catastrophic' birth and 'hospital-acquired disability.' Gabbard details the toll of his family's journey—from the harrowing, Kafkaesque foray into the 'bowels of American medicine' to unflinching, sometimes poignant, and often humorous scenes of caring for the boy, who becomes the North Star by which Gabbard grows as a person and as a father. This insightful account is offered in that very spirit—a fitting tribute to August's short but meaningful life—inviting the reader to ask 'what is personhood?' and to understand that we each have our 'own particular way of being in the world' and 'a right to remain' in it."

—LEZA LOWITZ, author of *Up from the Sea*

"Chris Gabbard's story of his son August's life will leave you thinking about fatherhood, modern medicine, philosophy, and the very definition of being alive and human."

—MARK WOODS, author of *Lassoing the Sun*

"Gabbard is a detective confronting the most wrenching of all mysteries as he attempts to make sense of the chain of medical errors and misjudgments that caused his son, August, to be born with profound disabilities. . . . Gabbard also writes with wit and humility about how caring for August prompted him to reexamine his deepest assumptions about the value and purpose of a human life. This book should be required reading for parents, caregivers, teachers and doctors."

—RACHEL ADAMS, author of *Raising Henry*

"This profound and profoundly moving book testifies to the soul-shaking power of unconditional love, which transforms a tragedy into a life to be treasured."

—MARK OSTEEN, author of *One of Us*

A LIFE BEYOND REASON

A LIFE BEYOND REASON

A Father's Memoir

CHRIS GABBARD

Beacon Press, Boston

BEACON PRESS
Boston, Massachusetts
www.beacon.org

Beacon Press books
are published under the auspices of
the Unitarian Universalist Association of Congregations.

22 21 20 19   8 7 6 5 4 3 2 1

This book is printed on acid-free paper that meets the uncoated paper
ANSI/NISO specifications for permanence as revised in 1992.

Text design and composition by Kim Arney

Library of Congress Cataloging-in-Publication Data
Names: Gabbard, Chris, author.
Title: A life beyond reason : a father's memoir / Chris Gabbard.
Description: Boston, Massachusetts : Beacon Press, [2019]
Identifiers: LCCN 2018043304 (print) | LCCN 2018047745 (ebook) |
ISBN 9780807060582 (ebook) | ISBN 9780807060575 (hardback)
Subjects: LCSH: Gabbard, Chris—Health. | Fetal
brain—Abnormalities—Complications. | Children with
disabilities—Biography. | Hypoxic-ischemic encephalopathy. | Father and
child—Biography. | Parents of children with disabilities—Biography. |
Medical errors. | BISAC: BIOGRAPHY & AUTOBIOGRAPHY /
Medical. | FAMILY & RELATIONSHIPS / Death, Grief, Bereavement.
Classification: LCC RG629.B73 (ebook) | LCC RG629.B73 G33 2019 (print) |
DDC 618.3/2680092 [B] —dc23
LC record available at https://lccn.loc.gov/2018043304

For Harriet McBryde Johnson
(1957–2008),
who gave me ideas

One doctor makes work for another.

—ENGLISH PROVERB

AUTHOR'S NOTE

I HAVE TRIED TO TELL THIS STORY AS ACCURATELY as possible. In most instances, names or identifying details about individuals have been altered to protect the identities of the parties involved. Names of medical institutions and a medical device manufacturer (and its products) have been changed. With the exception of Dr. Munodi, there are no composite characters. I have attempted to stay true to what people said and did, but all memoirs are by nature imperfect. They are so because, even if a memoirist is writing with the best of intentions, truth—when it is complicated, subjective, based on memory, and put into words—cannot be empirically accurate. Despite these drawbacks, I have written my son's story so that it will be preserved. If I didn't put it down on paper, it would be as though these events had never occurred.

A LIFE BEYOND REASON

1

"MY WIFE'S READY TO GIVE BIRTH," I SAID MEEKLY. "Where are the doctors?"

On the other side of the high counter at the nurses' station, a middle-aged blond woman was standing and gazing at a computer screen. When I approached, she looked up and said, "May I help you?" The clock on the wall behind her read 3:23. It was the morning of March 5.

It was nearly spring, in a more innocent time. At the close of trading that day the NASDAQ would reach halfway to its dot-com peak. I was still using a PalmPilot. Everyone was switching from AltaVista to Google. In three months Napster would launch, in five months Blogger. In nine months we'd be partying like it was 1999, which it actually already was, not to mention freaking out about Y2K. But the world was about to change. In eighteen months there would be *dot-com, dot-shit, dot-gone*. And in thirty months the Twin Towers would fall.

But for now, from San Francisco and Cupertino to the Silicon gulches, canyons, flats, and knolls across the nation, visions of a glorious high-tech future and the wealth it would create danced in people's heads. Nothing but good could come from the technology revolution. Many in the Bay Area and beyond dreamed this dream.

On March 5, 1999, a share of the Hippocrates Corporation of America (a pseudonym), the biggest manufacturer of medical devices in the United States, trading symbol HIPC, opened nearly two dollars over its previous day's opening. This company was the Apple Computer of the health-care industry, merging digital technology with medicine. The darling of Wall Street, Hippocrates was revolutionizing the way doctors treated patients. Quarterly reports indicated robust sales for its wonder drug Relaxanoid (a pseudonym), used to treat spasticity of cerebral palsy, and its implantable drug-infusion pump (the Relaxanoid pump) and other digital medical devices were generating astronomical profits. Owning a few shares ourselves, my wife, Ilene, and I loved the growth of the stock price, not realizing that our son, soon to be born, would one day have one of the company's devices implanted in his body.

The nurse looked up briefly. "Everyone's giving birth," she replied. Fecundity evidently wasn't confined to the stock market.

"Will the doctors be coming soon?"

"They're very busy."

"Oh, I'm sure they are," I said, apologetically. "I wouldn't want to trouble them. But I just want them to know that my wife is ready."

"Ready?"

"To give birth," I said, clarifying.

She looked at me quizzically. "It depends on what you mean by *ready*." Deciding not to debate the matter further, she continued, "I'll let them know. They'll be along. Don't worry."

Since she didn't ask me which doctors were ours or even who I was, I continued: "Dr. Latchesik is the attending physician. Dr. Atropski is the resident. I'm Gabbard. My wife is Chazan. We're in suite 1524."

She looked up again. "They'll come when they can." Then, giving me an encouraging wink before returning to her screen, she added "They'll get that baby out in no time."

I left the nurses' station and began looking for someone, anyone, to draw attention to our situation. I really wanted to find a doctor. In four months, I would become one myself. But I wasn't going to become *that* kind of doctor. I was just finishing my doctoral study at Stanford, focusing on the British literature of the Enlightenment, and getting ready to look for a teaching job. Of all the advice one of my dissertation advisors gave me, this was the best: "Never reserve a table at a restaurant in the name of Dr. Gabbard. You may find yourself in an embarrassing situation." What he meant was, if somebody were to go into cardiac arrest, it wouldn't help much to be a doctor of the epistolary novel.

The epistolary novel—fiction consisting of collections of letters—was a mainstay of the Enlightenment. This was not the enlightenment of the Buddha but the European Enlightenment of the eighteenth century, the movement that ushered in our modern, globalized world. I studied it in addition to the novel. Graduate students writing their dissertations, as I was doing during that period of my life, often become obsessed with their subjects. I tended to frame everything around me in terms of the Enlightenment and viewed all forms of progress as its legacy. In other words, I saw modern times as an extension of the Enlightenment. Think of the voice of Rod Serling of *The Twilight Zone* saying, "Imagine, if you will, a world in which the Enlightenment never ended."

Nothing epitomized the Enlightenment's lingering influence more than American medicine. This institution was the pinnacle of progress, a field where the application of human reason operated in its purest and most practical form. The Baconian empirical method incarnate, it had evolved exponentially over the preceding two centuries: anesthesia, penicillin, polio vaccines, laparoscopic surgery, mapping of the human genome, and progress against cancer. Birth had been made easier: In 1821 the Vicomte de Kergaradec was the first practitioner to recommend assessing fetal heart sounds for diagnostic purposes. And in 1853 William John Little was the first to argue that cerebral palsy stemmed from a lack of oxygen at birth. Given the centuries of linear progress and exponential medical advancement, no problem should arise regarding the simple matter of delivering a baby.

The trouble was, a problem *had* come up, but no one seemed to be available to deal with it. I turned corners, walking up one corridor of the fifteenth floor, where the maternity ward was located, and down another. The corridors were empty, yet the walls hummed with life. No doctor, nurse, or aide crossed my path, so I gave up the search. I had that feeling you get when you can't find your car keys. I headed back to the delivery suite, where Ilene and our friend Joanne were waiting. When I walked back into the suite, it was 3:25 a.m., and the only people there were Ilene and Joanne.

Thirty-nine hours earlier, on March 3, Joanne had made a comically grand entrance. She had barged into the birth suite exuberantly roaring "Whoopee!" and immediately followed this up with an even more exclamatory "CHILDBIRTH!" Midday Wednesday, Ilene and I were still fresh and able to laugh, having arrived just a few hours earlier.

Joanne Sasaki was a few years younger than Ilene and worked with her many floors below at Loma Prieta Medical

Center (a pseudonym). Like Ilene, she was a clinical professor of physical therapy. Joanne had short black hair, obsidian eyes, and a mischievous grin. She was Nisei. When dressed in her professional attire, she had a lot of tattoos that didn't show. She called Ilene *Crunchy* and me *Cowboy*.

Joanne was a hipster from our irony-rich neighborhood, our enclave of cheeky bohemian iconoclasts. She loved to talk about the internal workings of the body. She did this in ways that were so spiced with graphic detail that they made one feel a little queasy. One could be eating burritos with her, and she would launch into an anatomy lesson about the bowels, urinary tract, intestines, kidney, liver, or lungs. For this routine she used a deadpan voice, stating in an expressionless monotone all of the things that could go wrong with your body. This was a variation on "The worms crawl in, the worms crawl out," except that these were scary stories about our still-living flesh. It was as if she were taking the content of a medical textbook on pathology and turning it into material for horror stories to be told in the dark around a campfire. She could be a riot.

We lived in a time in which flippancy reigned. We approached the world with a jokey, mordant knowingness. This was another part of the innocence of the era—our smug assumption that nothing really serious could ever go wrong. We were living "with a mark on the door," as Ian Curtis of Joy Division had sung in "Passover," insulated from life's catastrophes, or so we thought. On top of everything else, we were completely unashamed of being silly. Our story at this juncture could have been titled, "What to Disrespect When You're Disrespecting."

"Welcome to our penthouse," Ilene said in response to Joanne's "CHILDBIRTH!" greeting.

"Hey, Crunchy," Joanne said, eyeing the fetal heart monitor. "I've a feeling we're not in Kansas anymore."

"I don't think I've ever been in Kansas," said Ilene.

Turning to me, she said in her faux Southern accent, "Hey, Cowboy, what's shakin'?"

"Not much," I said nonchalantly. "Just hanging out in our VIP birth suite. Is this cool or what?"

"Oh, man! It's huge!" Joanne exclaimed. "And look at that view!" Enormous windows made up two of the suite's four walls, and through them we could enjoy the bright expanse of downtown San Francisco in the noontime sun.

"It's—," Ilene started.

"Ginormous!" Joanne broke in. "It's almost as good a view as the one from Twin Peaks!"

We all paused a moment to take in the panorama as though it were a painting by Hokusai. A bright, hilly, street-strewn world presented itself. To the northeast, the great buildings of the city's downtown glistened like the white cliffs of Dover. In their midst stood the Darth Vader profile of the Embarcadero Center and the arms-akimbo Transamerica Pyramid. Beyond the skyscrapers were the cobalt blue of the San Pablo Bay and the gunmetal gray of the Bay Bridge. To the north, the top of one of the Golden Gate Bridge's reddish towers peeked roguishly over the crest of a distant hill.

"It's a room with a view," Ilene said from her reclining position.

"No," I quipped, "it's a *womb* with a view."

The bad joke provoked groans.

A day passed, and much more time would pass before we would see the sun again. It had last set at 6:06 p.m. on Thursday, March 4. We had not watched it sink into the

Pacific. To have seen that, we would have had to walk across the suite, press our right cheeks tightly against the glass, and peer westward over the full length of Golden Gate Park. Too preoccupied, we had instead settled for looking to the northeast. The downtown buildings had changed like chameleons from blazingly bright to burnished gold and finally to crepuscular gray. As the natural light had gone down, the city lights had come up. The buildings had soon glowed like beacons. And in the wee hours of Friday morning, they had continued to gleam, and a gossamer of streetlights had spread across the residential neighborhoods below. At 2:41 a.m., a gibbous waning moon had passed the meridian. But after that, over the next hour, the stunning cityscape had faded to black. When the lights of the city had completely gone out, the delivery suite's big glass windows had begun shooting back our reflections, as though we ourselves had become the spectacle.

Ilene and I started as a couple on the morning of January 15, 1991. We met in a San Francisco café called Tart to Tart. It's a dump now, but back in the day this place in the Inner Sunset was newly opened and smelled of wild strawberries. The Muni's noisy N Judah line streetcar ran outside the café's windows. At the time I was just finishing my master's degree, and I looked up from my books, papers, and espresso to observe a beautiful woman purchasing a latte.

Sequestered as I had been in Catholic schools, I had not met any Jews prior to my first year in college. But ever since then I had been particularly drawn to Jewish women. She was five foot three and had an hourglass figure, cute sexy walk, brown eyes, and curly dark brown hair tumbling below her shoulders. Her face was like that of a subject in a Charles Landelle painting. She carried her drink from the counter to a table on the far side of the café. Intrigued, I got up and walked over and said, "Are you going to work?"

She turned out to be smart and funny, and, I learned, her favorite color was periwinkle. She was the type of person who insisted on rearranging the luggage in the trunk of the car after I'd already packed it. She had grown up in Canoga Park, a city in the San Fernando Valley, and that meant she had once been a "Valley Girl." But at the tail end of her sentences there was no residue of the valley's legendary upspeak.

Over the next year I learned that Ilene's background was middle class. Her mother was Charlotte Orzoff; her father, Fred Chazan. Their ancestors had come to the United States in the first two decades of the twentieth century. The Orzoffs settled in Chicago after escaping from Tiraspol, a city in what is present-day Moldova, during the tsarist pogroms of 1903–1906. The relatives on her father's side, the Freiders and Chazans, fled from Vyshnivets in Ukraine in 1920. Following the Bolshevik Revolution, the White Russian army had carried out pogroms, from which her family had escaped. Four of her Freider relatives who remained behind— Sonia, Rachel, Yentl, and their mother, Hannah—would perish several decades later in the Holocaust. The Freiders and Chazans who came to America settled in Omaha before moving on to Santa Monica. Eventually Fred and his father (Fred's mother had died by then) settled at Venice Beach. Fred served in the military in Alaska right after World War II. Members of the Orzoff and Chazan families set up a mail correspondence between Fred and Charlotte, and after he completed his service the two met, married, and settled in Canoga Park, where they had two children.

Charlotte died when Ilene was nine years old of a kidney disease that today is nonfatal. She was only thirty-nine. Up until her mother's death, Ilene had been raised as a conservative Jew, but afterward her father stopped going to the synagogue, and this ended her religious upbringing. After graduating from UC Santa Barbara, she moved to San Francisco where she worked as a food server in restaurants such as Max's Diner and Dante's on Pier 39. She began studying to become a physical therapist, and in the fall of 1987 she flew "back east," as many westerners say, for graduate school interviews. It was while sitting in a glassed-in patio café in Quincy Market in Boston that she saw her first snow flurries. When I met her, she had recently graduated from Boston University with a master's in physical therapy and worked at the prestigious Loma Prieta Medical Center.

When we became engaged, Ilene had to call all of her Jewish relatives to tell them that she was marrying a man named Chris. It would have been a little easier if my name had been Moshe. We were married on the morning of August 1, 1992. Our ceremony took place before friends and family in a lovely garden under an azure sky. Steve Woodhams was my best man. Our Song, one that Ilene and I definitely did *not* have played at our wedding, was R.E.M.'s "Losing My Religion." No one at our nuptials but us would have understood why a couple so in love would have chosen this to be Our Song.

For the next few years Ilene and I lived the dream, taking evening strolls on Baker Beach and Saturday morning hikes on Mount Tamalpais, with weekend getaways to Carmel, Point Reyes, and Big Sur and two-week vacations to Lassen Volcanic National Park. Everywhere we went, we traveled with music, listening to cassette mixtapes. We were optimistic believers. Ilene believed in the good that science and medicine would bring. And I believed in the Enlightenment, the ideals of which had become my religion. That movement had laid the foundation of medicine and science and would allow humankind to control its destiny.

Our respective families also became smaller. The last time my father, Arvil, took unaided steps was on our wedding day. He died two years later. My mother, Fran, had passed away twelve years earlier. Ilene's father, who was well at the time of the ceremony, died of a stroke three years afterward. Each of us had only one sibling, both of them brothers, so we now were members of remarkably small families.

I'd been slow to warm to the idea of having our own family. I was not interested in what I had considered in my youth to be the false consciousness of family values. At one time, I'd been convinced that parental love for children was nothing more than bourgeois sentimentality or a primitive response mechanism. In high school, we called the girls who wanted to become mothers "baby makers." Moving to San Francisco as an adult, I commonly heard procreating heterosexual couples referred to as "breeders." I harbored a similar sort of antipathy to child-rearing. Individuals have a right to not have children if they didn't want them, I would think (and this is still my position).

When I was younger and people, such as my dad, suggested that I start a family, I'd think, *I'm no fool*. But he contradicted his own advice when another time he said, "If you want to accomplish anything in life, keep the kids off your knee." To be frank, I didn't like children. I didn't see any point to having them. I thought they were boring. They would ruin my life. You would have to pry my male independence from my cold, dead hands. All of which is to say, I was about as interested in having a child as I was in having a tumor.

In my callow confidence, I completely believed in my own judgment. Long before meeting Ilene, I had moved to San Francisco from Palo Alto because I thought that, beyond my hometown being rich in squirrels, absolutely nothing of any importance was happening there. I also had a number of pet idiosyncrasies. I found the phrase *spiritual journey* annoying (stories of spiritual journeys were packed with profundities without substance), hated films that were sentimental tear-jerkers (you couldn't buy me with sob stories), gravitated to alternative music (I only liked love songs that were ironic), and preferred living in a community where the sarcasm was clever and the pop cultural references frequent. I found that community in San Francisco before it became too expensive to live there. We in that community believed that people who didn't conduct their lives in the light of reason were, in my vocabulary at the time, "unspeakably stupid." Why couldn't people act rationally? We were constantly examining and reexamining our lives because we all more or less implicitly agreed with Socrates that "the unexamined life is not worth living."

But then I met and married Ilene, and the idea of being a dad began to grow on me. I decided I would do it ironically, which is to say playfully, with a jaded urban hipster's state of mind. I recall telling my buddy Steve, "I'm going to be a parent, but on my own terms." Perhaps I sensed it was time to move on from the Peter Pan phase. Regardless, in the middle of 1998 a home test strip reported positive, and becoming a father seemed to portend a flourishing world, a world of fullness. Fullness meant a lawn and flowers in the front yard, a white picket fence with a gate, and robins in the trees, a vision I'd glimpsed in David Lynch's *Blue Velvet*. Because we were living in a cramped San Francisco apartment, it was ironic that I had come to imagine fullness as a cool late-nineties upgrade of the "Gee, Wally" wholesomeness of the 1950s TV sitcom *Leave It to Beaver*. We were awaiting the arrival of Theodore Cleaver, Version 2.0, a child of the new millennium. Would *this* Beav emerge from the womb with tattoos and piercings?

Ilene fell in love with the baby from the moment she knew it was coming. It took me much longer to get to the same emotional place. I could have used another year without a baby. A line from the song "7" by Catfish and the Bottlemen comes to mind, one to the effect that I would love him but would need another year without him to get things done. In fact, I could have used another two or three. I had great things to accomplish. Specifically, I wanted to be the next Stephen Greenblatt, an internationally recognized American Shakespearean scholar, literary historian, and Pulitzer Prize–winning author. Or at least I aspired to be someone like him, someone who would shake up my field of study, British Enlightenment literature.

The choice for the hospital came down to two. California Pacific Medical Center, known locally as CPMC, a facility close to home, served the local community. Annually it performed three times more deliveries than did its chief rival, Loma Prieta. It was primarily in the business of birthing babies, and its name might as well have been Babies-R-Us. Outside of San Francisco, though, no one would have heard of it.

Loma Prieta was the other option. Ilene felt comfortable there because it was her place of employment. But more importantly it was an internationally acclaimed teaching hospital, universally recognized for excellence, employing the best and the brightest, one to which wealthy people from all over traveled to receive the best medical care. Few if any hospitals were more respected by health professionals than Loma Prieta. This was supposed to be one of the best hospitals on the planet. But perhaps this was the issue: the problem lay less with the hospital and more with the planet.

Our first glimpse of the boy was on a screen. Afterward we were handed a photo like an old-fashioned Polaroid print: a fuzzy black-and-white sonogram. The scene it captured resembled something you might see on the Weather Channel: a westward-moving hurricane just beginning to form off the west coast of Africa or near the Cape Verde islands. In the upper left corner appeared the date: *31 – JUL – 98*. In the upper right the words *LPMC PRENATAL DIAGNOSIS* and immediately below *PT: CHAZAN ILENE, SONO.*

Knowing it would be a boy, I began to dream about the things we would do. We would backpack in the High Sierras, where, camping in the wilderness, we'd drink in an ocean of stars while sitting beside a fire. We'd go to baseball games at AT&T Park, where I'd teach him to root for the Giants and against the archrival Dodgers, the way my dad had done with my older brother Jesse and me back when the team played in Candlestick Park. Maybe the boy would be a nerdy, geeky hipster like his dad, and when he was older he'd introduce me to new concepts or take me to see an independent film being screened for the first time or a cool new band to keep me up to date. Whoever he would turn out to be, and whatever it was he would enjoy, and whoever he would love, he was *so* going to be magnificent!

Ilene and I took all of the measures expected of enlightened parents-to-be living in a technocratic society. In preparation for this birth, we underwent genetic testing before conceiving, and Ilene had an amniocentesis early in the gestation period. All of the test results pointed to healthy development. Having read *What to Expect When You're Expecting*, Ilene stopped drinking coffee and alcohol, which she had never done much of anyway. Prior to and during the pregnancy she didn't take any medications, and before becoming pregnant she had followed the recommendation of taking folic acid supplements.

Our Inner Richmond apartment was very small—only six hundred square feet, but, with the San Francisco rental situation being what it was, we couldn't think about moving. The dot-com bubble was seriously bulging. We went about assembling baby supplies. Ilene's cousins Linda and Wes in Antioch lent us the crib that they had used for their kids. We placed a new changing table against one wall in our bedroom and purchased a bassinette. Friends threw a baby shower. We created a birth plan expressing our dream of how the birth should go.

The baby's due date arrived, February 20, 1999, a Saturday. By Monday, the baby had not come, but the medical staff with whom Ilene interacted never deemed her pregnancy to be high-risk, so we weren't worried. To pass the time, we attended a matinee screening of Terrence Malick's war movie *The Thin Red Line* at a theater in the Marina District. During the closing credits, Ilene sensed for the first time that the baby was not as active as it had been. In fact she felt no fetal activity at all and immediately suspected that something was wrong. After the movie she went to the office of her OB-GYN next to Loma Prieta, where the fetus underwent tests. Her OB-GYN was part of an all-woman practice. The nurse said the results didn't look good, the numbers were low and very worrisome, and so she told her to go up to the fifteenth floor of Loma Prieta. There a young male resident physician repeated the tests, carrying them out hurriedly. Ilene told me afterward that he seemed tired.

"Your baby is fine," he said when he was finished.

On Monday, March 1, ten days after Ilene's due date, the test results again were "not good." The numbers were troubling.

Yet the nurse conducting the tests said reassuringly, "Your baby is fine."

"Are you certain?" said Ilene.

"Absolutely."

"I think there's something wrong."

"Come back in two days and Dr. Klothoberg will oversee your induction unless you go into labor before then. All expectant moms worry too much. Everything will be all right. Come back in two days. We'll get that baby out."

On Wednesday, March 3, dawn awakened us to a day of great expectation. The sky was clear, the air was a crisp fifty degrees, and a gentle wind was blowing in from the west. Our world was radiant with sunshine. A good day to have a baby! Ilene and I assembled our things, drove across town, and parked our Toyota Camry high on a steep hill behind the hospital, curbing the front tires. After walking down the hill, at the main entrance of Loma Prieta Medical Center, we stopped. We were going to hatch a dragon egg. With great anticipation of the dragon adventure ahead, we hugged, kissed, and approached hospital glass doors so dark they seemed black. All that we could see as we walked up to them were our own reflections.

March 3 rolled into March 4. Joanne came and went, came and went. The doctors and nurses changed shifts, with Dr. John Klothoberg going off duty and Dr. Sandra Latchesik coming on as the attending physician. She was a slender white woman of medium height, maybe in her mid-forties, with very short, dark blond hair, large cheeks, wire-rimmed glasses, and blue eyes. Joining her was Dr. Lisette Atropski, who was younger, slightly shorter, with long, dark brown, flowing hair, tortoise-shell glasses, and a broad smile. She also was white. Atropski would be the physician who would be with us the most throughout the labor. She was warmer and more relaxed than Latchesik, but she also was diffident and spoke softly. So deferential was she that at first I mistook her for a nurse.

Dr. Latchesik, by contrast, was dominant, epitomizing complete self-possession and control. She was all business. Her area of expertise was perinatology, a subspecialty of obstetrics concerned with complicated, high-risk pregnancies. Every inch the expert, she made an almost imperceptible nod whenever she said something authoritatively, which was frequently. Standing with her back straight, wearing her starched white lab coat, she would assert something boldly and almost simultaneously nod, as if agreeing with herself.

As the attending physician, Latchesik was responsible for whatever the resident, Dr. Atropski, did. The attending popped in every few hours but would only stay a moment. She was a whirlwind. "She's not the most demonstrative of women," Ilene had said after her first prenatal appointment several months earlier. On a later occasion Ilene had characterized her as "an academic medical diva." I assumed this meant that Dr. Latchesik was one of the best and the brightest, and I didn't give this assessment a second thought.

One crew of nurses cycled off and another came on. A short African American woman in her mid-thirties became our main labor and delivery nurse. Busing in all the way from Sacramento, ninety miles away, she worked per diem, on a day-to-day basis. We never caught her name. As she went about her business, Ilene and I, and sometimes Joanne, watched the show beyond the big windows, the slowly shifting shadows of the tall downtown buildings. A little past midday on the second day a severe pressure pain began developing in Ilene's lower pelvis.

"I'm sure something is wrong," Ilene said. "It feels as if the baby's stuck, like it's impacted against my pelvic bone."

"Everything is going well," said Dr. Atropski. "That baby will be out in no time."

Ilene managed to take a few steps, but then the per diem nurse approached in a panic and hurried her back into bed— the electronic fetal monitor (EFM) indicated that the baby's heart rate was dropping. Joanne quipped, "Moonwalk aborted!" After settling Ilene back into bed, the per diem nurse insisted that everything was fine. She turned to the EFM, which was methodically churning out a stream of narrow paper, gathered up a stretch of it, and held it up. "This is where the baby's heart rate went down," she said, pointing, "and this is where the heart rate came back up."

Around 2:10 a.m. on Friday, Joanne temporarily left to retrieve something from her nearby apartment. Throughout the night and early morning, the pain in Ilene's lower pelvis intensified despite the epidural. She also had developed a fever, but at least dreaded preeclampsia was not an issue. It was 2:55 a.m. when the per diem nurse said to a second nurse, a young blond woman, tall and willowy, "The baby's heart rate is low." The two discussed whether the EFM was picking up the mother's heartbeat or the fetus's. Dr. Atropski joined in this quiet discussion and speculated that a problem was occurring with the EFM, not the baby.

"Must be Mom's," the resident said of the fetal heart rate. She then stepped out the door for about thirty seconds. The per diem nurse wasn't convinced. She seemed perplexed and asked the blond nurse again if the reading could have been the baby's. The blond nurse didn't answer. The per diem nurse then said, "These vitals are not reassuring. I don't believe the baby's heart rate should be this low. It's in the eighties."

"Must be Mom's," the blond nurse replied, repeating what Dr. Atropski had said. She spoke matter-of-factly.

"That doesn't seem right," the per diem nurse said. But then she dropped the matter when Dr. Atropski stepped back in and reiterated that the heart rate must have been the mother's. Atropski considered it a nonissue.

Joanne returned shortly after 3 a.m. Ilene was maximally dilated. Dr. Latchesik stepped into the room for a minute, a brisk encounter. Dr. Atropski told her then that a problem was occurring with the EFM. Latchesik didn't respond to this statement, and the resident physician didn't repeat herself. The attending physician obviously was in a hurry. Hours earlier, Joanne had dubbed her Dr. Dash Smoke because she'd been rushing in and out so much. Before dashing out, Latchesik suddenly shouted, "We're going to have a baby!" The exclamation seemed so out of character that I did a double take. Then she was gone.

Dr. Atropski, the per diem nurse, the blond nurse, and a third nurse we hadn't seen much of until then set up a sterile area and adjusted the bed from a sleeping to a delivery arrangement. They positioned Ilene on her back with her hips and knees maximally flexed. At 3:10 a.m. the EFM was removed. Ilene looked wretched and was still complaining about the pain she felt in her lower pelvis. I wondered why the epidural wasn't relieving it.

After these preparations, Dr. Atropski, the blond nurse, and the third nurse scattered to the hallway, leaving just Ilene, Joanne, the per diem nurse, and me.

At 3:15 a.m. the room grew eerily quiet. Then the per diem nurse said, "I'm going to check on something." And she scurried off too. Now Ilene, Joanne, and I were completely alone. Joanne and I exchanged glances.

"Are they supposed to leave us alone like this?" I asked her. "Is this typical?"

"I have no idea," said Joanne, "but I don't think it is."

In the forty-second hour of labor, Ilene was too worn out to add to the discussion. She was just lying there, breathing labored, facial expression locked in a grimace. These were things that profoundly upset me. I tried to soothe and console her, but my efforts seemed useless. Overall, though, I presumed that what was happening with her body—the pain she was in—was normal for a woman in labor.

More minutes went by. Joanne and I began to feel like passengers on a ship that has been abandoned by its crew. Then Joanne asked, "Where the hell did everybody go?"

Assuming that everything would turn out all right, I wasn't grasping how grave the situation was becoming. I just said, "I don't know."

"I wonder if the nurses and Dr. Atropski are trying to round up the pediatric team," said Joanne. "Cowboy!" she suddenly ordered, pointing toward the door, "go see what's happening!"

Her suggestion made sense. Go find help! As I was exiting I said, "Where should I go?"

"The nurses' station!"

She said this at 3:22 a.m.

The baby was born unresponsive at 3:44 a.m. A specially dispatched pediatric team had resuscitated the infant, bringing Lazarus back from the dead. A resident had held the tiny body up, a trophy of medical rescue.

Ilene, Joanne, and I had been thunderstruck. No one had spoken. No one had known what to say. I'd never before seen Joanne at a loss for words. But she had become speechless. Popular culture never mentions births that go badly, so there were no song lyrics or television or movie dialogue to reference about what had just taken place. We had gone off the media grid.

The newborn was whisked away to the intensive care nursery (ICN) on an upper floor of the hospital. Dr. Latchesik was gone. The birth had occurred less than fifteen minutes earlier, but already she had left. Other babies needed to be delivered. The hospital had rarely experienced such a high volume of births all at one time, so she'd had to race off to the next one, taking our main labor and delivery nurse (the per diem) with her.

Now it was 4 a.m., and the room was quiet. Dr. Atropski, a second nurse, and a third nurse we'd not seen much were performing the aftercare on Ilene. Joanne wordlessly helped me gather our things. She looked like a person dazed in the wake of a car wreck. As soon as we got the signal that Atropski and the nurses were finished, Joanne broke the silence, saying in a small voice, "We're done here." She then wheeled the suitcase containing unused candles and the forgotten birth plan, and I carried a bag with some belongings and held the string of the soccer ball balloon emblazoned "It's a boy!"

The recovery room was the opposite of what the labor and delivery suite had been. The luxury accommodation gave way to a dark, cramped cubicle. At this point, Joanne silently hugged us and headed home. Her work shift started on a lower floor in just a few hours.

Within forty-five minutes, Ilene and I heard a gentle knock. Two male physicians entered, Dr. Mellark and Dr. Kwok. Mellark began with the only good news there was: no meconium had been found below the infant's vocal cords. And then came the rest. Physicians use a method called Apgar, based on a 1–10 scale, to quickly summarize the health of a newborn, and an infant with a score of 8 or above is considered to be in good shape. Our newborn's Apgar scores were 2, 3, and 4 in the first ten minutes—abysmal.

"The infant has lost a lot of blood," said Dr. Kwok, "and so will need a transfusion, preferably with blood provided by one of the parents."

"Can you donate?" asked Dr. Mellark, finishing the other's thought and directing the question to me.

"Seizure activity has been noted," Dr. Kwok added. He asked us to sign a consent form for a lumbar puncture. This puncture, I found out later, would be just the first of three.

"The newborn's condition is critical," Dr. Mellark said. He didn't mince words. "The chances of survival are fifty-fifty." The odds shot around like a madly jumping ball on a spinning roulette wheel.

"You can go up to the ICN," said Dr. Kwok in a lowered tone intended for me, "but your wife should remain in bed to recuperate."

I attempted to sleep but felt agitated, so at a little before 6 a.m. I went up to the ICN. Ilene stayed behind, as Dr. Kwok had instructed. Alone in the elevator I felt lightheaded and weightless, a moment of extravagant sensory drift. Motion, thoughts, and objects became hard to untangle. I should have been plunging downward, but instead I was riding up. The elevator rose without stop, each floor gently dinging. The numbers swirled. The elevator came to a halt.

A broad corridor appeared, and beyond it was a set of white double doors. I approached, tested the door on the right, and found it locked. Then I saw the sign: Fogelman Children's Hospital. Visitors first needed to push a button and speak into an intercom. Once it unlocked, no one was on the other side of the door. Around a corner I came upon a bank of sinks beneath a mirror. A placard instructed visitors to scrub vigorously and then to don a gown, mask, and gloves. By the time I had finished preparing myself, a young nurse drifted up. Her scrubs bore a Peanuts theme, mostly images of Charlie Brown and Woodstock.

"I am Beatrice from the intensive care nursery," she said. "Let me take you down." And she started leading the way.

The corridor was empty and quiet, and her soft shoes made a faintly discernible squeak just loud enough to echo. The walls were a color somewhere between beige and pink, a color no one in heaven would select. A scent of cleaning solutions ghosted the air. Then we came to another set of white doors, and she pushed open the one on the right. Light flooded out, along with a patchwork of imperative but disembodied voices and a cacophony of alarms, buzzes, and bells, all of which sounded against a backdrop of low-grade thrumming. I caught a whiff of rubbing alcohol. Beatrice stood to the side, her back against the door to hold it open as I passed in front of her.

"Someone will speak with you in a moment," she said, and then she returned the way we had come.

Before me appeared the ICN theater, a large, long, rectangular room with a wall of north-facing windows at the far end. It was still pitch black outside. On the room's right side were an array of low, dark preemie tanks—translucent plastic, barely lit incubation chambers inside of which lay fist-sized existences curled up like sleeping cats. Parked along the left wall was a row of mostly unoccupied Isolettes.

Everyone was wearing surgical scrubs. No one came up to me; they were too busy. But then someone did stop long enough to point out where our baby's Isolette was.

I felt apprehensive. Considering what I'd witnessed two and a half hours earlier in the delivery suite, I expected to find an object as appealing as insect larva. I approached the Isolette like a first responder at a crash site, ready to have my stomach wrenched. Considering the baby's appalling color, I thought it would be better if he died. It would be better for his sake. It'd be better for our own. Ilene and I could try again for another, better baby. I would have been okay with that.

Critical-care personnel bustled urgently on the far side of the Isolette. Our baby lay within, utterly still. He was lying on his back with his knees bent, fists clenched, toes curled, and eyes closed. Everything about the baby's body was unbelievably small. Above towered an IV pole, from which dangled a bulging piece of futuristic fruit. A line snaked from the bottom seam down several feet to where it entered a motionless leg. A whitish translucent tube—thin as a hummingbird's beak—had been inserted into one nostril. The baby was breathing with the aid of a ventilator.

Save for the tiniest of diapers, his flesh was fully exposed. The earlier greenish-gray stillborn color had pinked up somewhat. Above the body, an extremely bright light radiated warmth. Only hours old, I thought sardonically, and already he was under an interrogation lamp. Electrodes covered his body, and a jungle of wires and lines relayed back and forth between the tiny form and several monitors and machines. An apparatus would occasionally sound an alarm, and someone would rush over to see what was happening.

Was this an infant? And was it ours, this wizened little creature? I took a quick survey. Eyes clamped shut and body not moving. Head was of seemingly typical size and shape for an infant but with a large laceration—a deep red impression on the forehead. The head must have been pressed firmly for a long time against some hard internal impediment. This must have had something to do with the pain Ilene had been feeling in her back during the labor, the pain the epidural couldn't alleviate. The abrasion was shaped like an ear. Why was it there? It was a mystery. I dubbed it "the mystery of the ear."

Overwhelmed, I lowered my head, closed my eyes, and took a deep breath. And then it happened. A sensation rifled through me as if I was experiencing some shamanistic, peyote-induced separate reality. I found myself mentally airborne, lifted up and propelled at breakneck speed through vivid images of distress. I visualized everything from the infant's perspective, forty-two hours in a matter of seconds. What had been in my mind a single, simultaneous, and coexisting image then broke apart and became a sequenced panorama, consecutive scene upon scene. And then I was spat out on the other side of this ghastly reverie into a new dimension. It was a terrain that was wholly unfamiliar—and a place from which I have never returned.

This hallucination couldn't have lasted more than a few seconds. But brief as it had been, my heart was afflicted as never before. I opened my eyes and looked again, but I couldn't believe what I saw, for the interrogation lamp had become a spotlight. The deep red impression on the forehead, the large laceration shaped like an ear—this injury was gone. And the wires, lines, and catheters connecting to the little body had vanished like visions in a dream, like things that disappear when we awaken. Now I could see clearly: the body was unencumbered, naked and free. It was luminous, and the little face glowed like a full moon. And in that moment I saw him for what he was. I was astonished, for he now appeared to be magically beautiful, the most amazing, radiant being I had ever beheld. In his tiny frame he encompassed the infinite and the eternal. An involuntary reaction—a primordial brain wave—flashed inside.

"My darling boy," I heard myself gasp.

WHEN INTERTWINED, LOVE AND GRIEF BECOME AS
ferocious as desire. My son was, in Keats's words, "full beautiful—a faery's child." His face also resembled mine in my
own baby photos. It startled me, since he seemed an exact
replica. He was like me, he was a piece of me, he was my
double, yet he was near death. I intuited what Emily Rapp
in *The Still Point of the Turning World* describes more eloquently than I could. She writes that the "great capacity to
love and be happy can be experienced only with this great
risk of having happiness taken from you." My darling boy
and I had hardly met, but already he was breathing on a
ventilator. His chances were fifty-fifty. And now he and I
both were trembling, in Rapp's phrase, "on the edge of loss."

"I want to see him *now!*" Ilene exclaimed when I returned
to the cubicle.

She was supposed to stay in bed, but now she wanted
to go and view for herself what I had seen. But she was too
sore to get out of bed. It wouldn't be for another two hours
that the two of us ventured out. She should have used a
wheelchair, but neither of us thought to look or ask for one.
Hunched over, she needed me to support her as she hob-
bled to the elevator. When we arrived at the ICN, natural

light was streaming in through the windows at the far end. We both approached the Isolette and looked at our new son. And there he was. We agreed that our boy was beautiful, so, so beautiful.

A senior resident physician approached, Dr. Lewis. I stood back now as Ilene took center stage, asking questions and probing for details. Having a medical background, she knew the terminology and grasped the meaning of the answers.

Dr. Lewis didn't know much. When the baby had been brought in over four hours earlier, no one present at the birth had sent word up describing what had happened. A car wreck had been delivered, but no explanation. He was attempting to do his best, and now he and the others in the ICN were trying to figure things out from scratch. He seemed frustrated that no information had been conveyed at the handoff. All he could say was that the baby had been started on phenobarbital. Beyond this, he was speculating wildly. He didn't know what had gone wrong at the birth, and he even suggested that the baby's condition might have resulted from herpes. "Herpes?" I asked him. "How is that even possible?"

We returned to our cubicle. Around noon a hospital staffer came by wanting to know what name to put on the birth certificate. We named him August David, taking the "A" from Arvil (my father's name) and the "D" from Ilene's father's middle name, David.

On Saturday, our fourth day since arriving at the hospital, friends and relatives began visiting. My brother Jesse and his wife Cristina came by to see the baby and lend support. By Sunday, August had stabilized and come off the ventilator. The main uncertainty changed from whether he would live to what his quality of life would be. By this point, we were not much surprised that he would be severely impaired; we had been surprised that he would live at all. That same day we had to pack up our things because health insurance wouldn't pay for us to board another night. Our tiny Inner Richmond apartment was a mile and a half away, on Twenty-First Avenue just south of California Street. When Ilene entered, she draped herself over the railing of the empty crib, weeping because there was no baby to put in it.

On Monday, August opened his eyes, which at the time were—true to the Celtic side of his heritage—unequivocally green. Then, like the waters of a hundred-year flood, the lines, catheters, wires, and tubes over the subsequent days began receding from his body. On Tuesday one of the nurses reluctantly showed us that his second and third toes on his right foot were slightly webbed together. She seemed to think that this would upset us. This was like learning that, in addition to the house being destroyed in a hurricane, one of the sprinkler heads was broken.

On Wednesday, a repeat EEG failed to capture more seizure activity, but it "did show flattened baseline." By then Ilene and I had begun to hold and bathe the baby and change his diaper. By turns he was floppy and rigid. On Thursday Ilene spotted on a table next to August's Isolette a nurse's index card. On it were scrawled the phrases "serious neurologic dysfunction" and "poor prognosis."

The hospital scheduled August for discharge on Monday, March 15, but before they could release him its representatives had to sit down with us. On the preceding Friday, we all assembled in a windowless conference room somewhere in the bowels of the enormous institution. This was the "family consult," one of a myriad of undertakings that the national accrediting organization—the JCAHO (formerly known as the Joint Commission on Accreditation of Healthcare Organizations, now simply the Joint Commission)—required of Loma Prieta. In situations like ours, the JCAHO compelled the hospital to supply representatives to meet with the family.

Green as an Oregon forest, I'd had high expectations going in, something along the lines of a graduate seminar. I pictured a systematic debriefing characterized by effective communication. I imagined that reasonable people without any vested interest would attend. Hospital personnel would respond forthrightly to our inquiries. All of the facts of the case would be placed on the table. Everything would be out in the open. Rational decision-making would be conducted in an atmosphere of complete transparency and neutrality. The scientific method would be on display.

As the meeting was getting started, I sensed that something was amiss. The two parties directly involved with the labor and delivery, Dr. Latchesik and Dr. Atropski, did not attend. And no one from the OB-GYN practice with which Ilene had undertaken her prenatal care was there. We wanted desperately to speak with them, but we were told that their busy schedules precluded them from being present.

Instead we met with five other hospital representatives, four male doctors, all wearing white lab coats, and a lone woman, a social worker. Two of the doctors we somewhat knew: we had seen the senior resident physician, Dr. Lewis, and the neurologist, Dr. Martin, in the ICN. The room seemed inadequately lit. Throughout the meeting everyone talked quietly, as though speaking in an old-fashioned library. Ilene and I sat on one side of a long conference table, and the four physicians sat on the other.

Beginning the proceedings was Dr. Martin. He had a reserved, understated style, and he spoke slowly and distinctly, emphasizing certain words, pausing between sentences, as though he was used to explaining difficult concepts. After making some initial remarks, he informed us that our infant had suffered a "hypoxic-ischemic brain injury." The term describing his condition was *hypoxic ischemic encephalopathy*. This was gibberish to me; he might as well have been rapping in Romanian. In a low voice Ilene translated for me. *Hypoxic* meant inadequate oxygenation of the blood. *Ischemic* meant a deficient supply of blood to a body part. *Encephalopathy* meant a malfunctioning of the brain. In sum, August had experienced a lack of blood and oxygen before or during the birth, and this had caused brain damage.

"The newborn," Dr. Martin continued, "sustained a brain injury consistent with asphyxia." As he spoke, his elbows rested on the top of the conference table. His hands alternated between clasping (as though praying), forming a steeple, and spreading out with palms up (as if checking for raindrops). He laid out the case that the infant had suffered a significant injury to his gray matter and the zone between the gray and the white matter. Elaborating, he used the phrases "watershed injury" and "dead zones." My mind stretched to the areas in the Gulf of Mexico that were said to be dead zones, where no sea life remained.

"Overall," he said, "his MRI showed diffuse injury throughout the cortex. The baby also experienced damage to the deeper brain structures such as the basal ganglia and thalamus."

"His cerebellum was undamaged," Dr. Thomson pitched in. He was a physician we had never seen before. I remember thinking that *cerebellum* sounded like *antebellum*. Was this supposed to be grounds for optimism? Ilene asked what all of this meant for the long term.

Dr. Martin answered: "Most likely the child will have developmental delays, potentially serious ones." Not everyone around the table was in agreement, however. Dr. Anderson predicted that probably, eventually, the boy would meet his milestones. Anderson was another physician we had not met.

"You believe he will meet his milestones?" Ilene asked, hungry for encouragement.

"Yes," Dr. Anderson said, nodding, "I do. I believe he will." The other three doctors shifted uneasily in their chairs. It seemed to me that they didn't agree, especially Dr. Martin, who cocked his head skeptically.

"How did this happen?" I blurted out, changing the subject. "Why did our baby come out this way?"

They seemed taken aback. Was I being impertinent? Dr. Thomson and Dr. Lewis exchanged a quick glance. It appeared that neither was going to touch the question. They were leaving it to Dr. Martin, who finally cleared his throat and said, "Things can happen in a pregnancy and labor."

"What kinds of things?" I said.

Dr. Martin was choosing his words carefully before saying, "A lot of hypotheses have been put forth."

"What are some of these hypotheses?" I said.

Again there was silence. Finally Dr. Martin said, "No one can say what happened."

"No one can say," I responded, "because you haven't found the answer? Or because you're not permitted to say?"

Dr. Lewis and Dr. Thomson again looked at each other. Dr. Martin said, "We don't know."

"Then when will you know?" I said.

"That's impossible to say," he said.

The four doctors and I were speaking at cross-purposes. I felt like a linguist trying to decipher the mysterious language of the heptapods. The gist of what they were saying was that what had occurred was an act of God, that these things simply happen. But I was suspicious of this explanation, seeing it as an evasion, and the exchange grew testy. After a little more back and forth, my voice rose: "Something is wrong here!"

"Whoa! Whoa! Whoa!" Dr. Martin shot back, holding up his hand and signaling for me to stop. "There was nothing that went amiss during the labor and delivery."

"I'm not talking about the labor and delivery, damn it!" I said. "I'm talking about the days leading up—" I was aware that I was attacking the wrong people. These physicians in front of us weren't to blame. Our beef really was with the doctors of the OB-GYN practice. They were the ones who had overseen Ilene's prenatal care right up to the moment we arrived at the hospital on March 3. Ilene, who knew that I could be a hothead, put her hand firmly on my wrist, signaling for me to be quiet. She would take over.

Following up, she asked about the two poor test results prior to induction but following the baby's due date of February 20. These were the ones conducted on Monday, February 22, and Monday, March 1, before she arrived at the hospital for induction on March 3.

Dr. Martin said that the two tests didn't indicate anything particularly worrisome.

"That sort of thing happens all the time," Dr. Thomson said, backing him up.

Ilene then asked about the poor test result of March 1 and the decision to postpone inducing labor until March 3.

Dr. Martin fielded the question: "Proceeding sooner wouldn't have made any difference."

"But if the baby was experiencing distress that early, as early as February 22nd and then a week later, on March 1st," she persisted, "and he was already eleven days overdue on March 3rd, he wouldn't have had the stamina to endure an excessively long labor and delivery."

"The labor wasn't excessively long," said Dr. Martin.

Ilene gasped. "Forty-two hours wasn't excessively long?" she asked.

But before she had a chance to continue her line of questioning, all four doctors began redirecting us toward focusing on the future. Now came a barrage of happy talk. There was a legitimate basis for it: recent research was showing the neuroplasticity of the brain and its capacity for adaptation to change, including structural reorganization following injury. This was a newer model, the older one having assumed that brain cells die due to injury, and then permanent loss of function follows. The new model gave grounds for anticipating improvement.

"Babies' brains are plastic," said Dr. Anderson, the one who had given us hope, saying that August might meet his milestones.

"Plastic?" I asked. I remembered a line from the movie *The Graduate*: "Ben, I want to say one word to you. Just one word: *Plastics*."

"Yes, plastic," Dr. Anderson said. "It's amazing what recovery can occur."

"Especially starting so young," Dr. Thomson said.

Ms. Cooper, the social worker, chimed in, "Getting him started with physical and occupational therapy is crucial. I will get you a referral for the Golden Gate Regional Center's

Early Intervention Program." Because of August's extremely serious condition, she went on to say, he would qualify immediately for the Medi-Cal waiver, known in other states as the Medicaid waiver.

On some invisible signal, the meeting started winding down. Dr. Martin leaned back and cradled his neck with his hands so that his elbows fanned up like wings. Looking like a bird in flight, he asked, "What are your plans?" A smile appeared on his face. It was the smile of reason.

"Our plans?" I thought about the future for a moment. It seemed that we didn't have a future. I felt like a man on a scaffold with the noose around his neck and the executioner asking, "What are your plans?" Maybe he was really asking, "Are you planning to sue?"

Finally I answered, "We plan to learn how to give our baby phenobarbital."

As if simultaneously hearing the same cue, they all rose. The meeting was over. It had lasted forty-five minutes.

Ilene and I never saw or heard from these five individuals again, save for Ms. Cooper, who secured the referral she had promised. Otherwise, this meeting was the last official contact we would have with the hospital regarding the birth, with two exceptions. One would be Ilene's postnatal visit with Dr. Latchesik roughly five weeks later. The other was the hospital's patient satisfaction survey.

It has been said that having a child with severe impairments is like becoming a member of a club you never wanted to join. Addressing this unwished-for membership is Emily Perl Kingsley, a writer for *Sesame Street*, who in 1987 published a short essay titled "Welcome to Holland." Before leaving Loma

Prieta with our significantly impaired newborn, a hospital social worker handed Ilene a copy. Kingsley writes, "'Holland?!?'
you say. 'What do you mean Holland?? I signed up for Italy!
I'm supposed to be in Italy. All my life I've dreamed of going
to Italy.'" Kingsley likens having a disabled child to arriving
in the Netherlands when you thought you were going to visit
Rome. "Welcome to Holland" has become a euphemism for
arriving in a place you would never want to go to but then
making the best of it. Kingsley's piece stresses the point that
if you spend your time grieving over not being in Italy, you
will miss what the Dutch have to offer. But the euphemism
is based on an analogy that doesn't make sense. Ilene and I
would have loved to be diverted to a place with windmills,
tulips, canals, cycling paths, and marijuana parlors.

A medical rescue team had resuscitated our son on the
brink of death. Now we were living with Lazarus. Diagnoses and labels for chronic and disabling conditions became
the small smooth stones on a string of worry beads: cerebral
palsy, spastic quadriplegia, profound mental retardation,
cortical visual impairment, microcephaly, seizure disorder,
osteopenia—and the list went on.

Despite all this, we loved our child very much, as most
parents would. But we also found ourselves in the unenvi-
able predicament of mourning the loss of what we thought
would be in the future—a "normal" boy growing into man-
hood. We felt intense shock, guilt, grief, depression, and
anger. We didn't progress from one of these feelings to the
next as with Elisabeth Kübler-Ross's stages of grief. Rather,
like the horses of a carousel, these emotions kept going
around and around.

Several people asked me if we were going to put August
into an institution, which was once the usual practice. Ilene

and I heard about another San Francisco couple with a similar baby who did this very thing, so we knew that institutionalization was an option. Still, in 1999 it wasn't common to commit severely impaired newborns to state institutions. This was what would have been done "back in the day," when poorly paid and overworked attendants would have treated him as something to be fed, washed, and put away again. The thought of August lying alone and abandoned in such a place would have been more than I could have borne.

On the other hand, we didn't know what we were getting into when we brought him home from Loma Prieta. All we knew when we returned to our apartment was that we had a schedule for administering anti-seizure medication. As if nothing had gone wrong, we sent out a chirpy birth announcement:

> Welcome • Bienvenue • Welkom • Haba • Bienvenido •
> Willkommen • Benvenuto • Salve
> August David Chazan-Gabbard
> Born March 5, 1999
> 6 lbs. 2 oz., 21 inches

Even before the snail mail notice arrived, many friends and relatives visited us in our cramped apartment. They came to hold the new baby and tell us how beautiful he was. But the gravity of the situation was not lost on them. They acknowledged this with their words, eyes, hugs, and support. We had officially named him August David, but almost instantaneously this name was supplanted by medical terminology, which attached to him and subsequently defined him.

"Welcome to Holland" doesn't take into account the psychological toll. "We differ from ourselves," writes Samuel

Johnson, "just as we differ from each other." Ilene and I now differed from what we once had been. Darkness descended, as though the moon had permanently locked into place in front of the sun, the start of a long eclipse. We grieved over losing what we had thought parenthood would bring. Ilene carried the burden of suspecting that she was responsible for what had come to pass. Because she had monitored her pregnancy closely and followed the expert advice, and because she had worked in hospitals, she felt that she should have caught the danger signs early. In the months following August's birth, a Mother Goose nursery rhyme kept going through her mind like an unwanted ear-candy jingle:

> *Humpty Dumpty sat on a wall*
> *Humpty Dumpty had a great fall;*
> *All the king's horses and all the king's men*
> *Couldn't put Humpty together again.*

The story of this anthropomorphic egg captured the gist of what had taken place. The dream of a happy, healthy child lay on the ground smashed to pieces

In times past, the fault for August's poor birth outcome would have been attributed to the parents. In 1569 Pierre Boaistuau wrote, "These monstrous creatures [are the result] of the incontinence & sinne of the parents." Vestiges of this assumption, what disability studies scholars refer to as the ancient symbolic model, linger into the present day. In a parallel vein, Ilene continually interrogated herself: Was there something she should have done or ought to have done differently? As she mulled over the personal "what ifs," there was another, far more existential one, an awakening to an atavistic struggle for survival. This circumstance becomes startlingly grotesque when the parties involved are a mother and her baby, but before modern medicine, nature frequently pitted these two against each other. Mary Powell, the wife of the seventeenth-century poet John Milton, died three days after giving birth to their daughter, Deborah, due to complications. Back then infection, hemorrhage, blood clots, preeclampsia, and obstructed birth were common causes of the mother's death in childbirth. Sometimes both sides lost. Katherine Woodcock, whom Milton married four years after Mary's death, died less than four months after giving birth, probably also from complications associated with the delivery. The baby died too. Such events must have been frequent. A late-fifteenth-century marble funerary relief by Andrea del Verrocchio, in the Bargello Museum in Florence, depicts two scenes. On the right is a woman dying during the process of childbirth, surrounded by grieving female attendants. On the left the midwife gives the deceased baby to the father in the presence of onlookers. The *Bargello Relief*, in the words of Elaine Hoysted, who writes the blog *Renaissance Mothers*, presents "one of the most the harrowing and realistic depictions of the realities of childbirth in art."

Before August's entry into the world, Ilene never dwelled on the subject of childbirth in such gruesome terms. But afterward, having viscerally experienced it herself, she awoke to the spectral presence of death that always lurks in the background of the birth process. In addition to the "what ifs" of how she had conducted her pregnancy, in this realm she also mentally played a macabre game of mother-and-baby Russian roulette, imagining various birth scenarios, each new one more appalling than the preceding one.

Because Ilene construed events in this particular way, she suffered a version of survivor's guilt. Why had she come out okay while her son had lost nearly everything? A person could have questioned her as to whether this line of thought was reasonable and productive. What good was thinking in this way going to accomplish? Probably she was clinically depressed. When bad things happen, people have to process the event in whatever ways they can. In this new dark world into which she had been unwillingly thrust, productivity and reason had become merely elaborate ways to dodge the actual issue, which was her earnest desire: "My little child, please come home."

In late April, roughly six weeks following August's birth, Ilene went to one of her regular postpartum checks with the physicians in her OB-GYN practice. Assignments rotated through the all-female practice to handle patient visits, so Ilene hardly ever saw the same clinician twice. On this occasion, however, she met with Dr. Latchesik, the physician who had supervised the delivery. As noted, she was a perinatologist, a doctor trained in the subspecialty of obstetrics concerned with the care of the fetus and high-risk or complicated pregnancies. Such a doctor is supposed to be highly skilled in prenatal diagnosis.

It was the first time Ilene had seen Dr. Latchesik since the morning of the birth. During the visit, Ilene asked about her prospects for having healthy children in the future, and the doctor indicated that she should have no problem. The likelihood of going through such a calamitous birth experience a second time was extremely slim.

"It would be incredibly bad luck," said Dr. Latchesik, "for *that* to happen again."

Bad luck. So the catastrophic birth was attributable to bad luck. This indeed was helpful because it was accurate. Who could deny that what had happened was bad luck?

However, as a woman of science, Ilene didn't find this explanation satisfying. Dr. Latchesik might as well have announced that our boy was a *lusus naturae*—a freak of nature.

⸻

August was so small, just a peanut, our "little bug," and so it was hard for us to imagine that he wouldn't always remain easy to care for. But we weren't facing facts. We didn't want to sue the hospital because we believed that only greedy, litigious people did that sort of thing. Having grown up in a family earning its living through a small business, I inherited the prejudices of that class, one of which is a deep-seated animosity toward lawyers. My buddy Steve reinforced this sentiment when he said one day, "You're not going to sue the hospital, are you?" But my dissertation advisor at Stanford, John Bender, told me to seek counsel. And he was far from alone.

A Bay Area group, Support for Families of Children with Disabilities, assigned Ilene to a mentor, Betty Lituanio, and Betty laid it on the line in the strongest possible terms, recommending to Ilene that we needed to take legal action *now*, not for ourselves but for August. He would require a great deal of financial support just to survive. The cost of his care over his lifetime, depending on how long he lived, easily could run into the millions of dollars. We needed to litigate on his behalf. He was the plaintiff, not us. If our son had been treated wrongly, it was his parents' duty to seek justice.

Friends and family members began advising us that we were heading into an extremely rough future. The expense of caring for August down the line would become exorbitant. There would be the need for medications, therapies, treatments, surgeries, wheelchair-accessible vans, and around-the-clock attendants. There would be the need for adaptive equipment such as a hospital bed for the home, a lift, and pricey assistive devices. There would be the need for home modifications such as the widening of doors and installing wheelchair ramps, both outside and inside the house. There would be the need to reconstruct a shower to accommodate a wheelchair user and the caregiver bathing him. There would be the need for a lifetime supply of diapers. Right now, they warned, he was small, cuddly, and relatively manageable. But in time he would grow, and his needs would overwhelm us.

While still in the ICN at Loma Prieta, August had been enrolled in a BAMRI (birth asphyxia MRI) study. As a baby born with a brain injury, he had undergone an MRI, and the team associated with the study conducted follow-up examinations. This team would eventually be instrumental in developing the CritiCool control unit, a device that reduces brain swelling in asphyxiated infants via a cooling cap. These would come online roughly ten years after August's birth and become standard protocol. In other words, August was born a decade too early to take advantage of this breakthrough.

At the six-month mark, the first week of September, the BAMRI people showed up at our apartment and had no sooner begun their tests with August than they began packing up their tools. They didn't say why, but I knew. August had the brain waves of a Stone Age boy. Socrates's dictum "The unexamined life is not worth living" came to mind. For the first time in my life I asked myself if this supposedly universal truth was really true. There was no way in the foreseeable future that August would be able to examine his life. Did this mean that his life wasn't worth living?

About the time that the BAMRI people visited, a new question arose. Should we medicate, or should we not? The doping effects of the antiseizure drug had to be weighed against the risks he ran if he didn't take it. August had so little going for him that we didn't also want to deprive him of the joy he took in living. But we also didn't want him to die from a seizure or suffer further brain damage. We made a decision. After a number of months, we slowly weaned him off of the medications, and by the last week of September he was drug-free.

For those outside of our household, August's vocalizations were mere noise. At one end of his sound spectrum was the category Ilene and I labeled *Les Misérables*. I learned to detect the varying qualities of his crying by pitch and duration. At the other end was the utterance that brought to mind Hélène Cixous's 1975 article "Laugh of the Medusa." This piece of poststructuralist feminist theory took on new meaning for me. Either August could remain trapped by a language that did not allow him to express himself or he could use his body as a way to communicate. To claim an identity truly his own meant vocalizing in a mode beyond the confines of the Western rhetorical tradition. And that's what the laugh of the Medusa was: his voice.

He also made a sound we called "the cry of the blithe pterodactyl." This was the call of a prehistoric bird soaring high in the azure sky, ascending to heights well beyond comparison with any mundane skylark of Percy Shelley's imagination. A full-throated and high-pitched shrieking suggestive of Bacchanalian ecstasy, it exhibited a sheer vitality that assured us that August was living in the warm precincts of a cheerful day. The loud, grating cry was the guffaw of anti-reason, of living contentedly in the moment, of enjoying life for what it was rather than always busying oneself with an improvement project. Hearing it, I would think, "Hail to thee, blithe Spirit!"

In October Ilene resumed working at Loma Prieta in the physical therapy department. After she went back, the doctors and administrative staff avoided her. The tension was palpable, she reported. Everyone knew what had taken place, and it seemed no one felt comfortable. At this same time August went to day care. The Child Care Center at Presidio Heights (a pseudonym) was a large, well-run facility, and it was directly associated with Loma Prieta. The staff seemed loving, nurturing, and knowledgeable. "August is a delightful spirit," said Ada, the lead provider and a young Russian émigré.

By this point I had finished my doctoral work and was teaching composition courses as a postdoc at Stanford. Almost every day I commuted thirty-plus miles one direction, so Ilene usually transported August to day care in the morning. In the late afternoon, she and I took turns picking him up. Every afternoon one of us would carry a portable car seat into the day-care center and then transport him out to the car in it. Often we would find him lying on the floor prone in the center of a U-shaped Boppy pillow (the kind sometimes used for nursing) and contentedly playing with a toy. When either Ilene or I approached and spoke to him, he almost always would acknowledge our voices by raising his head and giving us a big smile.

Over time we noticed that some of the parents of the other children at Presidio Heights were not comfortable with August being there. He was toddler age, but already he was perceived as different—as bearing stigma—because he couldn't toddle. These parents didn't want their children to be exposed to someone like him. I am reminded of a line from the cartoonist John Callahan: "Sorry. We can't have anyone this grotesque in here." No more than a young child, August already was ostracized. In these parents' eyes our little boy was the miniature equivalent of the Elephant Man.

These parents wanted to shield their children from "life's harsh realities"—meaning our son—assuming that he would frighten their kids. But the only harsh reality was the fact that he frightened the adults, not the kids. He became for these parents, as poet and memoirist Lucy Grealy says, "like some Dickensian ghost, imagining that [his] presence served as an uneasy reminder of what might be." The children, though, weren't put off at all by August. In fact, at Presidio Heights two little girls his age, Rachel and Isabel, regularly fought over which of them would have the privilege of taking care of him. For them he was a big living doll, but Rachel's mother didn't like this and so asked the staff to keep her daughter away from our son. That left Isabel. Over the span of many months, the staff members took about two dozen photos of her playing with him. In one she is putting her arms around him and giving him a full body hug, pressing her heart fully and tightly against his. She has large, sad eyes, like one of the big-eyed waifs in a Margaret Keane painting.

August's light-and-sound-emitting toys, the kind meant for children up to one year in age, proved as engaging for him as video games are for teenagers. One of the smaller expenses associated with his care was the cost of double-A batteries, which his vigorous play wore down at a breathtaking pace. When we secured him onto his Tumble Forms wedge on the floor and placed one of these toys in front of him, he used his left hand to flail at it with abandon.

The Tumble Forms wedge was a positioning device that consisted of a firm cushion covered in thick, dark-sky-blue plastic. In side view it resembled a gigantic doorstop. After laying August down prone on it we would strap him into place with two broad cloth-backed Velcro straps, each permanently attached to a side. The straps made sure that he wouldn't fall off the wedge to one side or the other or slide down the slope. His head would protrude over the top edge, and his arms would dangle over the top too. If we placed a toy on the floor directly beneath his head he could reach down and play with it even though he couldn't see it (on account of his poor vision). Sometimes while strapped onto his wedge August would squeal with delight and jostle his legs vigorously up and down for minutes on end. He was like a swim-lesson child holding the edge of a pool and learning to kick.

One late afternoon at Presidio Heights Ilene came as usual to pick August up and transport him back to the apartment. When she knelt down beside him and said his name she found he wasn't responsive. His eyelids were fluttering, with the iridescence of a dragonfly's wings. She hurriedly packed him into the portable car seat, ran out with him, and hauled ass through the two and a half miles of rush hour traffic to the emergency room at Loma Prieta. The ER immediately admitted him, but the nurses had difficulty inserting an IV. Finally one of them got a "stick" into his leg, a physician administered a powerful anticonvulsant, and the seizure abated. From beginning to end, August must have been seizing for at least an hour. He was checked in and spent the night, and the next morning he underwent a CT scan. Later that day, after viewing the results, one of the physicians commented to Ilene about what he saw. August's brain "looks like Swiss cheese," he said, "it's so full of dead patches."

Ilene and I subsequently feared that this big seizure might be a harbinger of more to come. It had been a few months since we had weaned August off of phenobarbital. Another repercussion of the seizure was that the administrators and staff at Presidio Heights didn't want him to return, fearing that he would have a seizure and suffer further harm, for which the facility would be liable. Their concern was genuine and understandable, so Ilene and I put August back on anti-seizure medication, administering it ourselves in the morning and evening. This didn't change their minds, though. Even with the possibility of seizure reduced nearly to zero, they refused to reconsider. With the exception of Ada, the lead provider, the staff members who previously had been so warm began emphasizing how fussy August had been, how difficult to soothe when upset. They also began insisting that they weren't nurses and so were not equipped to take care of him. When we received a final determination letter, we had to consider what to do. If the day-care facility associated with a major hospital wouldn't take him, no place would.

"We're terrified something might happen," said the chief administrator.

And that was it. This was fear speaking, not reason: fear of the unknown. Once the condition for which August was being excluded had been addressed, the fear should have diminished, but it didn't.

Ilene and I had no choice but to file a lawsuit. By this point we had already entered the dark, pugilistic world of litigation. Months earlier we had interviewed Allan Lerch, a brash pit bull of an attorney who had a deep, booming voice. This meeting was for the purpose of retaining an attorney to sue Loma Prieta Medical Center for malpractice. We signed a document with the verbal understanding that he would ask our permission before making any big moves. But within days he launched a scorched-earth, take-no-prisoners attack. Without first asking for our consent, having an outside medical expert review August's birth records, or undertaking anything of a discovery process, he filed a lawsuit for an astronomical award—millions of dollars in damages. So squeamish were we about suing that we fired him. Doing so turned out to be a huge mistake; his bare-knuckle approach was just what we needed, but we didn't know that at the time.

Months later, to get August reinstated at Presidio Heights, we hired attorney Cynthia Godsoe of the Child Care Law Center in San Francisco solely for the purpose of getting our son back into Presidio Heights. With her help we invoked the Americans with Disabilities Act (ADA), a wide-ranging civil rights law prohibiting discrimination based on disability. The ADA mandates that if "reasonable accommodation" can be made, then it must be made. The law established no ombudsmen or enforcement mechanism, however, beyond the lawsuits individuals bring against businesses and institutions refusing to comply. Some people perceive such lawsuits under the auspices of the ADA as get-rich-quick schemes meant to hurt small businesses. For us, though, this was hardly the case.

Godsoe made a few phone calls and filed some paperwork, and long before the case went to trial a compromise was worked out. August would be reinstated, and, under the Medi-Cal waiver, Presidio Heights would be supplied with two special chairs for him to sit in, and he would receive funding for a dedicated aide. As a consequence, August enjoyed full inclusion, and a Presidio Heights staff member, Veronica, a woman in her early twenties, was reassigned to become his full-time aide. If the ADA had not been in place, and had we not threatened to sue, this compromise would not have come about, and our lives would have been very different.

The ancient Greek poet Sappho wrote, "There is no place for grief in a house that serves the Muse." One day Ilene pointed at August and said, "Look, he's cracking up."

It was late on a weekday afternoon in February 2000. August was almost a year old, and just that day Ilene and I had set up house in our new place, a second-story flat on Fourteenth Avenue between Clement and California Streets in the Inner Richmond. It was a move of just seven blocks, but our new home, while older, was much bigger—nearly fourteen hundred square feet compared to six hundred. Our landlords, Hazel and Cathy Fong, had helped by giving us a significant discount on the rent for this other property they owned.

I was breaking down the cardboard boxes we'd used to move our things, kicking them open with my feet. It was a noisy job, and August was positioned on the living room floor nearby, strapped atop his Tumble Forms wedge. Something about the sound of collapsing boxes must have greatly amused him. He was in the throes of the biggest, most immoderate laugh imaginable: his head was up and thrown back, his mouth a big O. He was laughing so hard I was afraid he might hurt himself. In the years to come we found that he liked the sounds of dogs barking, door hinges squeaking, and, on Christmas mornings, the sound of the wrapping paper crinkling. He particularly loved the sound of jingling bells.

It was while living in this flat that I came to appreciate how much August loved his Mulholland stander. He spent a great deal of time in it. The stander was a piece of assistive equipment allowing a person with no muscle control to be positioned in an upright, weight-bearing posture. Whenever he was strapped into it, he looked as though he was standing up straight, and being vertical was good for his digestive system. The bottoms of his feet settled on a metal horizontal platform three inches above the floor. On the device's underside were wheels, so I could move him around while he was standing. When I rolled him through the flat, he beamed and sometimes squawked.

Imagine setting a small stone statue on a low platform with wheels. Or picture some visiting dignitary on parade—think of the Popemobile motoring slowly up a crowd-lined street with the pontiff standing and waving. This was August as I propelled him through the apartment. The difference was that, instead of waving as a pope would do, August would throw his head around, emitting toddler shrieks of glee and gesticulating drunkenly with his left arm. Humble as these journeys may have been, for him they were Mr. Toad's Wild Ride.

We toured our long stretch of two-bedroom flat as if we were sightseers. We slowly advanced up the carpeted hallway, around the dining room table, in and out of the kitchen with its ancient cracking linoleum, and then onto the living room's aging wood floor. Like foreign travelers we drank in the panorama beyond the big picture window, the evergreens across the way, and, through foliage, the traffic of Park Presidio Boulevard heading toward and from the Golden Gate Bridge two miles to the north. Before this magnificent view we would linger, me peering out, reflecting; he giggling, eagerly waiting to resume our holiday. Still in the honeymoon phase of fatherhood, besotted with my little boy, exploring this separate reality, I would rouse myself to resume rolling him forward. Our Mr. Toad's Wild Ride again underway, we were like two tourists on a big day out, eager to engage in whatever adventure came our way.

When August had just turned two, an electricity crisis was unfolding. Rolling blackouts were darkening California on account of the shenanigans of the now-defunct Houston energy firm Enron. It was a little past noon one day, and the power had just gone out, so I couldn't work at my computer. In our Fourteenth Avenue flat I would often park August in his Mulholland in the dining room next to my computer. The device came equipped with a belly-level play surface twenty inches wide and fourteen inches deep, and while standing he would play with toys. The tray consisted of thick, clear plastic like Plexiglas, around three sides of which was a half-inch high lip protruding upward to keep toys from falling off. As a game, I would load the tray with about fifteen plastic and metal balls slightly bigger than golf balls, and around the stander on the floor I would position six or seven large metal bowls to catch the balls when they fell off the tray. The balls would make a big sound when they landed in the bowls.

August's left hand, the semi-usable one, would feel about on the surface of the tray before him, probing to capture a ball. When he would finally pick one up, he'd bring it to his mouth and sample it with his tongue and lips. This was his way of experiencing the world.

Often he would have trouble grasping the balls, and as his hand hunted for one it would send them rolling over the tray, making a noise. The noisier they were, the more engaged he would become, so the faster he'd move his hand around, trying to capture one. Soon they were scattering like billiard balls. One finally would shoot over the tray's lip and into one of the bowls below. A zinger! The sound of the ball hitting metal and circling around the bowl would startle us both. He would stand completely still, seemingly stunned by what he had done.

After a brief pause he would resume playing again, enthusiastically rolling the balls around on the tray. Another eventually would go over the side, followed by a high-pitched reverberation.

"Goal!" I would yell, and he would laugh.

This had become our sport, our way to play ball together. It wasn't that he knew what the word *goal* meant, he just liked the percussive chime of the ball hitting the bowl and me shouting the word. Then he would be back at it, furiously rolling the balls. After a few seconds another would go over the tray's lip, followed by another metallic clang.

"Goal!" I would cry again, and at this he would laugh very hard. I would begin to laugh too because he was so amused, and then he would laugh even more. I loved watching the way delirious joy overcame him, the manner in which he would throw his head far back, the way his body convulsed, his eyes half closed and his mouth agape.

After firing the scorched-earth attorney Allan Lerch, Ilene and I selected another lawyer, Kevin Domecus, for our malpractice suit against Loma Prieta. He was young and relatively soft-spoken, and he initially seemed eager to take our case. After spending over a year in the first phase of the discovery process, reviewing the birth records in consultation with an outside medical expert, he decided to withdraw. He didn't tell us why, but by this point we had begun to do research and had discovered that California is a "capped state."

We were learning about how litigation works. If we were going to take legal action, whether to obtain monetary damages or just information, we were going to run into the brick wall of the Medical Injury Compensation Reform Act, or MICRA, which had been signed into law in 1975 by Jerry Brown the first time he was governor. It was the doctors' lobby and the insurance companies that pushed for passage of this legislation. Presented as a measure to limit frivolous lawsuits, MICRA had imposed a cap on pain-and-suffering damage awards, one that may have been reasonable back in the 1970s. This was one of the first laws of its kind, and many states now impose similar caps. However, the California legislature had never adjusted the cap for inflation, and so over time it had become a draconian limitation. Lawyers taking birth injury cases do so on a contingency basis, meaning they don't require litigants to pay a retainer in advance. Rather, they accept a fixed percentage of the recovery (the amount of money the defendant pays to the litigant) should the suit be successful. In other words, lawyers' fees come out of the assets the court awards. In doing so, however, attorneys are taking a risk, because litigating a birth injury case can cost them hundreds of thousands of dollars. As a consequence of MICRA, which severely limited what they could be paid out of the recovery, lawyers in 2001 were walking away from such cases even if they had a reasonably good chance of winning them. "Reasonably good" was not good enough: the profit margin had become too thin, and an attorney had to be almost certain of victory to take on such a case.

In early July 2001 I interviewed attorney number three. Her office was located in Opera Plaza near City Hall. The brother of an old girlfriend, a successful attorney living in Tiburon, assured me that Nina Buchanan was a good lawyer. A principal in the firm Buchanan & Buchanan, she was in her early forties and a native San Franciscan. During our talk, she gained my full confidence, and in her presence my doubts and apprehensions vanished. She had studied law at the University of California, but mainly it was her smile, naturalness of character, and casual humor that won me over. That afternoon I turned over to her our only copy of August's birth records, a seven-inch-high stack of documents. Three and a half years would elapse before we would have possession of it again. This was a mistake—we should have made our own copy so that we would have had it to consult. But at the time this didn't seem necessary. Buchanan & Buchanan, we assumed, had a vested interest in winning our case.

Within forty-eight hours of what would be my only meeting with Nina Buchanan, she commenced the discovery process by sending a copy of August's birth records to a physician to review, someone, she assured us, who wouldn't know the chief defendant, Dr. Latchesik. This individual would play the crucial role of outside expert for our court case, going meticulously through the birth documents to determine whether malpractice had occurred. Buchanan stressed that it was important for this person to be impartial and that he should have no relationship whatsoever with the defendant. She selected Dr. James Baelish, an OB-GYN and perinatologist who at that time was working at the UCLA Medical Center. Los Angeles being four hundred miles to the south, this should have guaranteed that this outside expert would not have known the defendant. Or so we thought.

Then we waited. As 2001 rolled into 2002, Buchanan delegated our case to a newly hired junior member of the firm, Byron Greyscale. "Byron is extremely good," she heartily assured us by telephone. "And I will oversee everything he does." After that we communicated with Byron by phone, mail, and email. Then, in late 2002, Dr. Baelish reported to him that malpractice undeniably had occurred. By then Ilene, August, and I had moved to Jacksonville, Florida, so Byron had to fly across country to meet with us. On an unseasonably warm Sunday in early December, he came to our house. This was our first conversation with him in person. His purpose was to prepare us for the following Monday and Tuesday, which were likely to be two grueling days of depositions. We would be placed under oath.

A product of a prestigious midwestern law school, Byron was in his late thirties. He was tall, slender, and handsome, and he was self-assured in the way trial lawyers often are. He, Ilene, and I sat around a circular table beneath a large umbrella on our deck. Even in its shade we started to sweat.

Byron got down to business. The one thing we knew for certain was that the baby at birth suffered from hypoxic ischemic encephalopathy. Several times, though, Byron inadvertently revealed that he didn't have a strong grasp of the facts. Ours was a difficult case, he said, and coming up with a successful strategy would be a challenge. "An adverse event occurred," he surmised, "but the question is, at what point?"

Byron disclosed that Dr. Latchesik had stated under oath in her deposition that it wasn't until 3:33 a.m. on the day of August's birth that she first learned a serious problem had developed. At that time the problem had, in her words, "already begun." The technical term for the problem, he explained, was *bradycardia*—meaning low heart rate. When bradycardia is detected, doctors have thirty minutes to get the baby out, often by cesarean section.

"You mentioned something in an email about a per diem nurse?" Byron asked. "There's nothing in the records about this nurse. You say that the hospital brought her in for the day?"

"Yes," I said. "A temp worker. She'd bused in from Sacramento. On Thursday afternoon—"

"Wait!" said Byron. "She came from Sacramento?"

"Yes. That's what she told me. She told me she'd boarded a bus early that morning, Thursday morning, March 4th, to take this day job. She said it was a two-and-a-half-hour ride, door to door. She was our main labor and delivery nurse."

"I remember her," said Ilene. "She was attentive. She was the one who had me get back in bed when I was walking. That was the night before the birth, Thursday night. The baby's heart rate had dropped."

"Exactly," I said. "That's when Joanne made a joke about 'Moonwalk aborted!'"

"A low heart rate may indicate asphyxia, a lack of oxygen," Byron said as he furiously scribbled notes.

Ilene said, "The nurse showed us the strips." The electronic fetal monitor (EFM) spat out strips (sometimes called tracings) that provided a record of the fetal heart rate, which was stored in both digital and paper form. The hard copy version was the birth's paper trail. "The nurse wanted to re-assure me," Ilene continued, "so she held the strips up and said, 'This is where the baby's heart rate went down, and this is where the heart rate came back up.'"

"Funny, there's nothing about her in the records," said Byron. Then he changed the subject. "Oh, yes, by the way, speaking of the heart rate, you said in an email two weeks ago something that she'd said to you about the fetal heart monitor?"

"No," I said, clarifying. "The main nurse—the per diem—said something about the monitor to the other nurse, not to me. And she said it early the next morning, March 5th."

"By the other nurse, you are you referring to the second nurse?" said Byron, wiping beads of sweat from his forehead.

"The tall blond one," I said. "A slender wisp."

"I haven't deposed her yet, so I don't know what she looks like. What did the per diem nurse say to the main nurse?"

"Wait! No!" said Ilene, clarifying once again. "You have it wrong. The per diem *was* our main labor and delivery nurse. The blond nurse, she wasn't the main nurse. She didn't have enough experience to be the main nurse. She was very young."

"Okay. This per diem was the main nurse," said Byron, finally getting the lineup straight. "Boy, doesn't it seem odd that they'd bring a temp worker in from Sacramento to be the main nurse?"

"They must have been short-staffed," Ilene speculated.

"So," said Byron, "the per diem nurse said something very early Friday morning to the blond nurse about the monitor?"

"Yes," I answered. "I remember her checking the reading for the monitor and saying to the blond nurse, 'The baby's heart rate is low.'"

Byron scribbled a note on his yellow legal pad. "That's interesting," he said, nodding. Suddenly he seemed excited. "There's nothing in the records about this. What happened then?"

"Dr. Atropski stepped over and conferred with the per diem and the blond nurse," I said. "They spoke quietly, but I overheard the doctor tell the two nurses that the reading 'must be Mom's,' meaning Ilene's. The fetal monitoring device was picking up the mother's heartbeat, not the baby's. Then Dr. Atropski stepped out of the room for a moment."

"Then what happened?"

"While Dr. Atropski was gone, the per diem—"

"And she lives in Sacramento?"

"Yes. That's what she told me. She'd ridden the bus from Sacramento. She was African American. Short. Maybe thirty-five years old. Maybe forty. The per diem wasn't convinced about the monitor reading," I said. "She thought that the reading *had* to be the baby's. The blond nurse repeated back to the per diem what Dr. Atropski had just said, you know, 'must be Mom's.' And the per diem said, 'That doesn't seem right. These vitals are not reassuring. The baby's heart rate's in the eighties.' Or words to that effect."

"The eighties is below the acceptable range," observed Byron. "A normal range runs between 110 and 160 heartbeats per minute. If doctors detect fetal distress, meaning a heart rate above or below the range, they have a maximum of thirty minutes to get the baby out."

Ilene nodded, and I said, "Check."

"So, then what happened?"

"Then Dr. Atropski returned to the room, and she repeated to the per diem nurse that the heart rate must be Mom's."

"Wow!" said Byron, staring off as if he'd spotted a smoking gun hovering in the sky like a dirigible. "And what happened then?"

"That was it," I said. "The monitor reading wasn't discussed again. The doctor settled the matter."

"Well, did they readjust the monitor to get the baby's reading?" asked Byron.

"I don't know," I responded. "I don't remember. I didn't realize at the time that this stuff was so important."

"There's not a thing in the records about a per diem," he repeated. "I didn't see her mentioned. The hospital didn't disclose it. I'll have to go back through the records and look again. When did all this happen, the talk about the monitor?"

"I don't know," I said. "It was a blur. At the beginning of the third day. Friday. Early."

He sipped his cold drink and continued, "Can you estimate a time?"

"Well, no. I don't know," I said and thought for a moment. "Forty-five minutes before the birth maybe? Fifty minutes? It wasn't an hour. I really can't say. I think it was before 3 a.m. Right before. It was so quick. I didn't think anything about the heart rate at the time because Dr. Atropski didn't think anything of it. 'The doctor must know,' I thought."

Byron took a moment to reflect. "Ilene, do you remember any of this?"

Ilene shook her head. "I remember something vaguely. By then I was drugged and uncomfortable. I wasn't myself."

"So, I'm the only one who remembers this?" I asked.

"Well, yes, you," replied Byron, "and maybe the per diem nurse, and the blond nurse, and Dr. Atropski."

"And Joanne Sasaki," I added.

"Yes, of course, Joanne," he said. "I may have to go back to Dr. Atropski and put her under oath again."

"Do you think that this heart monitor issue is important?" asked Ilene.

"I don't know," he said. "Fetal heart monitors are notoriously unreliable. They're so unreliable, they're hard to build cases around. I've seen more than one crater."

"The main thing, from my point of view," Ilene said, "is that they waited two days to induce labor, from March 1st to March 3rd."

"Yes, I know. I'm looking at that."

"Why did they wait to induce?" she wanted to know.

"That's what I'm thinking," he said.

"The test on February 22nd indicated the baby was already in trouble," she said. "Waiting so long means he didn't have the stamina to endure the labor and delivery."

"No," he agreed. "Obviously not. But the real question is, how and why did an experienced practitioner fail to detect a major problem in the delivery room? That's the question we have to answer." Later, as we were walking him out the front door to his rental car, he said by way of parting, "We're going to hold these people accountable!"

We gave our depositions on a top story of a high rise, the Bank of America building in downtown Jacksonville. We could see for miles out the big windows. Byron and the Loma Prieta attorney questioned Ilene and me individually, Monday for her, Tuesday for me. Six months pregnant, the poor stenographer tapping away at her machine at the end of our conference table had to record Ilene and me as we recounted the story of our child's horrific birth.

On Tuesday, my day, Byron was still looking for an angle. Some of his questioning focused on the fetal heart monitor. For the record I repeated my recollections of what the per diem nurse had said regarding it.

Several weeks following the depositions, we received word that a trial date had been set, November 8, 2004, a long way off.

Eighteen months later, a letter from the law firm of Buchanan & Buchanan arrived. It was dated June 28, 2004. Byron was informing us that he and the firm were no longer going to pursue our case. Evidently Dr. Baelish, the outside expert reviewing August's birth records, had looked at all the evidence again and realized that he had made a mistake. Initially he had thought that the birth had taken place at 4:10 a.m., but now he saw that it had occurred at 3:44. He concluded that hospital personnel had acted quickly enough once they'd determined that our son was experiencing distress. One sentence in the letter baffled us:

> Dr. Baelish re-reviewed the heart rate tracing and believes that the heart rate seen on the heart monitor tracing is Ilene's and not August's.

We didn't dwell on this information because of what came next:

> With all of the evidence establishing that August was delivered within 10 minutes of the bradycardia, we cannot establish that [the hospital] was negligent in its care and treatment of you and August.

Byron was saying that Dr. Latchesik and Dr. Atropski knew at 3:33 a.m. on the morning of March 5 that August was in trouble, and they got him out by 3:44 a.m. They delivered him in eleven minutes, and that span of time was within the thirty-minute window, so the hospital was not at fault.

Ilene and I were floored. We knew that we were in real trouble. We didn't have our own copy of the birth records, so we had no documents to consult, just our own imperfect memories. From the letter's brusque tone, we felt that we could ask Byron only one more question, so we responded by inquiring why the hospital had waited two days to induce labor, from March 1 to March 3. We were fixated on this period prior to induction. We kept going back to the error that we suspected the OB-GYN practice had made leading up to labor and delivery. This was our faulty premise, our own idée fixe, from which stemmed a chain of bad reasoning.

Byron didn't immediately reply. In fact, it was almost two months before a response came. What we received arrived by snail mail. The letter was dated Tuesday, August 24, 2004. It was his last communication with us, and it was uncharacteristically short:

> According to our expert, there was nothing below standard about any of your pre-natal care, including the decision to wait to induce labor. Our expert does not think that any of the tests done before admission required immediate induction.

It was clear now what was happening. Dr. Baelish had tossed so much cold water on August's case that Byron and the firm were dropping it. The firm obviously didn't want to risk throwing good money after bad by paying a second outside expert to review the records.

I had not appreciated at the time just how much MICRA was hamstringing August's case. I knew about the law, but I didn't take it sufficiently seriously. The popular prejudice that birth-injury lawyers made an incredible amount of money was one I shared. I'd even supported MICRA back in 1975 when Jerry Brown signed the bill. I too thought it was a good idea to clamp down on frivolous lawsuits. The idea that this law might come back to bite our family in the future never occurred to me. Now, in the early 2000s, I just figured that Byron stood to benefit so greatly that he would somehow find a way to win. What I didn't know was that the limitations this law imposed made Buchanan & Buchanan's profit margin far slimmer than I had assumed. Byron and the firm had to be absolutely certain of victory or else walk away. Any difficulty at all looked like danger. This was how MICRA influenced August's case—it drastically cut into what an attorney could earn, and so he or she could not risk losing cases. It was a matter of remaining in business. From Byron's tone in the letter, it was clear that we should just accept the outside expert's finding and let the matter go.

After our dealings with Byron, at least with regard to the legal realm, the rest was silence. Silence, that is, except for the holiday cards that arrived every winter for the next seven years from the law firm of Buchanan & Buchanan.

III

"GIVE HIM A SIBLING."

When Ilene and I asked August's Loma Prieta pediatrician, Dr. Han, what would be the best thing we could do for our son, this was what he said.

By 2001 Ilene was pregnant. We were booked to fly east early on July 5 to move permanently to our new home in Jacksonville. My goal had changed from becoming the next Stephen Greenblatt to securing a tenure-track teaching job of any kind and ASAP, one offering health insurance. Ilene and I would need it to cover August's enormous medical needs. We couldn't wait for a settlement to cover these expenses. There weren't many openings in my field (British Enlightenment literature), and I had to take the first permanent position I could get. It turned out to be at a young school, the University of North Florida (UNF). What it lacked in national profile, it made up in curb appeal.

On July 5, 2001, Ilene, August, and I boarded a plane in San Francisco on the first leg of our journey to our new home. The moment we left, we started referring to California as *the old country*. Five months pregnant, Ilene had to put up with the intense heat and humidity of the summertime south. The baby was due to arrive on Halloween, and immediately Ilene set to work making contacts to find an

OB-GYN practice. She settled on St. Luke's Hospital, just off Butler Boulevard near I-95, for the birth. Because of August's disastrous entry into the world, the medical staff there immediately deemed her pregnancy to be high-risk.

Before moving there, I had hardly ever thought about Florida. In California you don't dream about moving there in the way you might if you live in the Northeast. Once we arrived, I started getting the lay of the land. From the Florida Keys up as far as Orlando, they say you have to drive north to get to the South. Jacksonville was the informal capital of lower Georgia. It had been the hometown of one of America's great writers, James Weldon Johnson, and a pocket of Yankee urban hipness was tucked away in its Riverside neighborhood. The massive St. Johns River cut through the middle of the city. It narrowed considerably as it progressed northward through the urban center, made a hard right at the base of the downtown, and eventually emptied into the Atlantic about fifteen miles to the east. The city itself was midsized, attractive, affordable, and easy to navigate. Life was easier there than in the old country.

We bought a home on the east side of the St. Johns River in the San Marco neighborhood. Upscale shops lined San Marco Square, where a large fountain with three big bronze lions stood in front of a Starbucks. More than half a mile south was Craig Creek, a little stretch resembling a mini Louisiana bayou. Fingering in from the river, this primordial swamp was fronted in places by cedars, the roots of which projected upward like stalagmites. This swamp is said to be home to alligators, but only once have I seen one there.

Two-thirds of a mile south of Craig Creek was the home we'd purchased. It was one of the cheapest and smallest houses in an affluent neighborhood of older residences. A dense tree canopy draped with Spanish moss shaded the streets. After decades in a city, I was going to live in a place where the buildings weren't on top of each other and the yards were bigger than postage stamps. The neighborhood was well-heeled, with scrupulously tended yards of harmonious landscaping and sumptuous lawns. The river was very close, and bordering it were the posh mansions of Alhambra Drive, a few of them resembling mini Versailles with high walls and gated entrances and Land Rovers and Jeeps and Jaguars parked in the long driveways leading up to them. Our house, a block inland, and far more humble, had been built in 1938 by Truman Capote's uncle, and young Truman had spent several summers there. Around the corner from us would live the grandniece of Harper Lee. During the sale the mortgage broker, an elderly gentleman, referred to Ilene as the "trailing spouse." As we were leaving his office I said to her, "Toto, I've a feeling we're not in San Francisco anymore."

Later in the summer, Ilene hired a doula named Janet. Ilene had learned the hard way that delivering a baby was too fraught, too momentous an occasion to be left entirely to doctors. At first I balked at the expense, but she persuaded me to go along. She said that we could no longer trust that physicians would "look out for us."

Ilene had another good reason for hiring Janet. She wanted a doula to assist her in avoiding a repetition of what went wrong the first time by having a natural childbirth. Wishing to remain clear-headed and vigilant, she planned to go through the ordeal without an epidural. It wasn't that she was being ideological; that is, she wasn't trying to be an earth mother by having a pure childbirth experience. Rather, she just desperately desired to give birth to a baby with all of her brain cells intact. A healthy birth the second time would go a long way toward undoing the psychological damage she had incurred from August's birth.

As we were preparing for the birth, 9/11 happened. That morning Ilene was checking out a school for August to attend, and all of the television sets there were tuned in as she walked through the classrooms. I was at home feeding August breakfast when she called, exclaiming, "Our country is being attacked!" In the days and weeks following, to protect her maternal ecosystem for the baby's benefit, she stopped watching the news.

On the morning of November 1, Ilene and I headed for St. Luke's. My aunt Agnes Gabbard from Arkansas and Kathryn ("Kat") Grifo, a college student and August's chief caregiver, stayed home with our son. For the second time in our lives Ilene and I stood at the threshold of a hospital, having stopped to hug and kiss. This would be our second dragon adventure. And again we approached the hospital's dark mirror doors, seeing only our own reflections.

The OB-GYN, Suzanne Swietnicki, welcomed the doula and cheerfully worked alongside her. Throughout the labor Janet assisted Ilene with breathing exercises and other techniques. And Ilene managed to go through the process entirely drug-free. The baby arrived after nine hours of labor at 7:11 p.m.

We had no idea that the process could go so smoothly. We immediately grasped another difference. When a mother giving birth receives pain medication, the drugs infiltrate the infant's system, and this makes the newborn dopey. This infant, though, didn't have any drugs circulating in her blood, so her little coffee-bean eyes popped open immediately, and within minutes she was an alert, beady-eyed baby. In fact, she was staring at us.

That evening we gave her the name Clio. We pulled out the birth plan from two and a half years earlier. Among the "Other Requests" listed in it had been the desire for "immediate bonding with the baby after birth." We had hoped for "the baby to be placed on mom immediately after birth to allow for skin-to-skin contact." This time the request could be granted. A full moon began rising at a little after midnight.

August's blithe pterodactyl shrieks mingled with the sounds I heard when dropping him off at the Mt. Herman Exceptional Student Center. Each morning, I would drive six miles northwest on I-95, crossing the Fuller-Warren Bridge spanning the St. Johns River and skirting the western edge of downtown. Just off Eighth Street, it sat on the opposite side of I-95 from UF Health Shands Hospital. Once parked, I would wheel him in the front door and sign him in with Miss Beverly, the front-desk secretary. It was a short walk from there to his classroom.

The first day, I was overwhelmed to see so many medically fragile children assembled in one place. The student population was about 160, and a number of them had tracheotomies, feeding tubes, and oxygen tanks, and lived with severe cognitive impairment, cerebral palsy, blindness, and other conditions. Three full-time nurses had to be on the grounds to attend to their medical needs, and they were never idle. Every year, one or two students died—sometimes more—from natural causes, always at home, never at the school. That first day I found not just the sight but also the soundscape distressing, with its cacophony of idiosyncratic noises, the screeching and squawking. That our son would be included in this population was devastating. My heart sank.

This feeling didn't last, though. I soon settled in and, before I knew it, was seeing the world anew. The squawking and screeching, I quickly learned, were cheerful sounds. Despite their problems, these were kids just being kids, doing silly kid things. Mt. Herman turned out to be a wonderful school for August. Its teachers and administrators showed good morale and strove to do excellent work. The teachers who couldn't handle the situation quickly transferred out, while the ones who stayed became deeply committed to serving the students.

Many of Mt. Herman's teachers remained even though they were penalized for choosing to work in this school. No way existed for them to earn the bonus that Florida rewarded its teachers whose students showed sufficient progress according to certain metrics. They remained because they were dedicated to the school's mission. Mark Cashen, the school's inspirational principal, and the Mt. Herman teachers treated August with dignity and never gave up on him.

Again Ilene and I weaned August off the antiseizure medications, and this time we had far better results. Afterward he experienced only minor and infrequent seizures, ones lasting for up to twenty seconds at most and occurring months and sometimes years apart. Such short and infrequent ones did not threaten his health.

In February 2002 a three-track CD of Winnie the Pooh songs appeared in our house. It had accompanied a diaper promotion. One day I popped it into the CD player. August was on the playroom floor secured onto his Tumble Forms wedge, a larger one now because he had grown a little bigger. When the music began playing, he threw his head back in a roar of delight. The CD's opening song was "Winnie the Pooh," with a lush chorus of voices, and after it finished August settled down. I played the opening track again, wondering what was up, and when the first strains burst forth, he once again threw his head back and chortled so hard he could barely breathe. August loved music! Over the years he developed other favorites. He particularly enjoyed Dan Zane's "All Around the Kitchen," Raffi's "Bananaphone," the Muppets' "Life's a Happy Song," and Oscar the Grouch's "I Love Trash."

August also loved Cocoa, a pony. Riding this small, cream-beige-and-gray horse provided extraordinarily happy moments beginning in March 2002 and continuing for at least four years. Every Monday in the late afternoon (except in winter), I drove him to a large, fenced-in, grassy field now owned by Jacksonville University in the Arlington neighborhood. There, for thirty minutes a week, he underwent hippotherapy with physical therapist Lisa Federico and her volunteers. By this point we had tried myofascial release, acupressure, cranial sacral work, and sensory stimulation (we avoided hyperbaric chambers, which turned out to be of questionable value). At least with hippotherapy, we found something August liked immensely.

"How's Augie going to ride a horse?" asked his wise pediatrician, Stephen Cohen, when I asked him to sign a form allowing him to participate. August riding a horse would require three people to assist, I told him. One would place a thick four-inch strap with two large handles around August's middle (a handle would be on each side). Next they would hoist him onto Cocoa's back. Lisa would take the bridle while two volunteers, one on each side, would walk along and hold onto the handles so that August wouldn't fall off. The horse's motion made him giggle, beam, and crow. For thirty minutes, the four humans and the horse would saunter around the field's fenced perimeter like Chaucerian pilgrims journeying toward a distant shrine.

In late July 2001 August started going to the DLC Nurse & Learn in the Murray Hill neighborhood under the auspices of its early intervention program, of which there were remarkably few in northeast Florida. In March 2002, when he turned three, he "aged out" of early intervention, as is typical for such programs. Just at that time our finances required Ilene to start working again as a physical therapist. It was easy to find a good child-care arrangement for Clio, but having a kid such as August was like having an elderly parent with Alzheimer's disease and needing 24-7 care. We had to find coverage for the after-school hours, the days school was not in session, and holiday breaks. Day-care facilities wouldn't accept him. If you go to IKEA and wheel your severely impaired little boy to its Småland play area, no staff member there is going to let him in. Ilene began looking for a day-care facility, but August was completely shut out. And there was no equivalent to Cynthia Godsoe of the Child Care Law Center to help us. Fortunately for us, the DLC Nurse & Learn was willing to accept children with severe impairments into its regular day-care program.

In the years to come, the DLC was where August would go every day after school and all day during the summers. Whenever August was there, Ilene and I could relax, knowing that he was in caring hands. Amy Buggle, the founder and chief administrator, and her staff treated him with respect and loving attention, recognizing his dignity as a human being. If it had not been for the DLC, Ilene or I would have had to stop working and stay home, and this was something we could not afford to do. The DLC proved to be a great boon because it allowed parents and guardians

of children with severe and multiple impairments to continue working.

When August was born and for several years afterward,
his condition did little to challenge my belief in reason and
progress. I never doubted that, were I to dig down deeply
enough and be granted access to all the facts, the question
of what had happened to him at his birth could be answered. At first this rationalistic stance served me well, for
I remained confident that the world was ultimately explain-
able. On some level everything still made sense. Of course,
I still had to wrestle with the reality of August's physical
and mental state. On account of his catastrophic birth he
was a spastic quadriplegic (cerebral palsy paralyzed almost
all of his body), lived with cortical blindness (the cortex
could not process the images coming from the optic nerve),
was profoundly cognitively impaired, and was nonverbal.
He also was incontinent; he would forever wear a diaper.
He could take food and drink by mouth, but he could not
use his arms, so Ilene and I had to deliver every spoonful
of food and sip of liquid to his lips. We could have had a
feeding tube implanted (a G-tube) and saved ourselves the
trouble, but he *so* loved to eat that we did not want to deny
him this pleasure.

When we were feeding him, he could not just sit in a
chair the way that a typically developing child would. He
needed upper trunk support, so he had to be secured in his
wheelchair with straps holding his shoulders and chest in
place. Propped upright, his head lolled, falling forward and
backward: the muscles in his neck never developed properly.
He also drooled, and this occurred because the spasticity

affecting his mouth prevented him from being able to swallow his saliva efficiently. When he was lying on the floor, he was unable to crawl, scoot around, hold himself up, roll over, or even touch his toes. If someone were to put him in one spot and leave him, he would be found in the same location an hour later, give or take a few inches.

Overall, I continued to believe that the unexamined life is not worth living. But blebs of doubt had begun forming in the glass of my worldview, and eventually secure assumptions started to give way to questions for which no answers seemed possible. Why had everything gone wrong at August's birth? Why was my beautiful boy so impaired? Why was he so deprived of the basics of life? Why had this calamity happened to him? And beyond these questions concerning the past were others about the future: Who would take care of him after Ilene and I died? Most importantly, how would I ever find peace, knowing that terrible things had befallen my boy?

Like a strong wind at my back, the force of these questions began to propel me forward in a new, unexpected direction. I found myself increasingly grasping for something. Were I to miraculously receive all the answers about August's birth, find the empirical truth, the scientific basis, would this really make a difference? That my boy remained nonverbal, non-ambulatory, visually impaired, and diaper-reliant was a reality I had to face. But science and reason couldn't help me do that. Because they provided cold comfort, a bigger problem was at hand. I began to suspect that modernity—heir of the Enlightenment—this brave new world, was hollow at the center. There was no *there* there. It offered nothing but incessant change and vague promises of a better tomorrow.

And so I, the least likely of pilgrims, suddenly found myself embarking on a spiritual journey, that category of narrative that I as a young man had dismissed. My Enlightenment clockwork universe lay shattered on the ground, and I had to ask myself, *How did I get here?*

My father's ancestors were Scotch-Irish and had been living in America since the early 1760s. As a young man, my father, Arvil, migrated penniless from Arkansas to California, where he met and married my mother. Later he spent time in jail, two years in Soledad Prison, for passing bad checks, or so I've been told. This event took place when I was too young to understand or remember, and I didn't learn about it until I was twenty-eight. After being released, he worked for many years as a hardware store clerk before opening a business that sold parts for irrigation systems. Raised a Protestant, he was a nonbeliever, but he went to church anyway to please my mother, Fran.

Fran's people on her father's side came from the Azores and had lived in California since the 1850s, and her mother had emigrated from County Mayo in Ireland. Later in life, my grandmother would send a check every month to the Irish Republican Army. Born and raised in Palo Alto, my mother grew up in comfortable circumstances because her father had done well in local real estate. She was a stay-at-home mom and a devout Roman Catholic, as were all of our relatives on her side of the family. A few of them were priests, and Fran and her Irish kin hoped that I would become one too. I attended St. Albert the Great Elementary School and served as an altar boy at St. Thomas Aquinas Church. I thought seriously about going into the seminary—this was when I was eleven and twelve. So invested in Catholicism was I that I regularly read Fred McCarthy's cartoon *Brother Juniper.* I presumed that sainthood was in my future.

Instead of the seminary, I went to high school at the closest one to Palo Alto that was Catholic, Saint Francis High in Mountain View. I had to ride the Southern Pacific train every morning to get there. My mother insisted that I attend Saint Francis even though nationally acclaimed Palo Alto High School was one block from our house at the corner of Coleridge Avenue and Alma Street.

The Brothers of the Holy Cross ran Saint Francis, named for the twelfth-century pacifist of Assisi, Italy, and it was then an all-boys school. Now it is co-ed and prestigious, a premier institution in Silicon Valley, with Google headquartered a little over three miles away and Apple less than six. When I attended, the so-called seat of human progress (Silicon Valley) had not yet developed. The town of Mountain View was sleepy even though a number of major companies, such as Hewlett-Packard and Lockheed, were located in the region. In the not too distant past, the area had been devoted to growing prunes. Many of my classmates sprang from newly flush second- and third-generation Italian American families that had sold their prune orchards to developers, who replaced them with subdivisions and office parks. The student body consisted of about eight hundred, only one of whom was African American, a fellow the other students called Animal.

It was the school's dean of men, the head disciplinarian, Brother Patrick, a man in his late twenties, who propelled me down an unexpected path. His anti-Semitic views were well known, and he was aware that I didn't agree with him, but I'd had no idea where he really stood. I thought he might have just been playing devil's advocate. But one time in a private conference in his office (I was being castigated for some minor infraction), the subject of the Holocaust came up. In the midst of what had become a heated discussion, I pointed out (triumphantly, or so I thought) that the Nazis had lost the Second World War. To this he responded, shouting earnestly, his face red with passion, a vein popping in his forehead, "WE GOT RID OF THE JEWS, DIDN'T WE?" I immediately understood that he was no devil's advocate but the devil himself. He wouldn't have become viler in my eyes if he had suddenly sprouted horns. It had never occurred to me that a Roman Catholic man of the collar could be a rabid neo-Nazi. A lot of things can change a young person, and I remember many things that altered my course, but that meeting in Brother Patrick's office stands out. It was a major blow to my faith.

The last straw came in my senior year when I encountered the problem of theodicy, the question of why God allows innocent children (and others) to suffer. One day a teacher, Brother Marco, a kind, elderly, and cultivated man (and definitely not an anti-Semite), brought an eight-line poem into class from Archibald MacLeish's play *J.B.*, which loosely tells the story of the biblical figure Job. This poem captured the conundrums of theodicy: If the universe was created and is governed by a good, just, and loving God, why does he let evil prosper? Why does he allow pain? Why does he permit innocent children to suffer? To my adolescent mind the whole thing seemed illogical. If doctrine didn't make sense, God must be a fairy tale. My faith unraveled, and I lost my religion.

It was about this time that I watched Kenneth Clark's monumental *Civilisation*, a BBC-produced thirteen-part television documentary series that aired on PBS. On our local affiliate it was constantly repeated, a favorite rerun. It outlined the history of Western art, architecture, and philosophy since the Middle Ages. I was particularly intrigued by the tenth episode, "The Smile of Reason," which shed favorable light on the Age of Enlightenment.

One document Clark mentioned was "*Was ist Aufklärung?*" ("What is Enlightenment?") by the late-eighteenth-century German philosopher Immanuel Kant. In it, Kant defined *enlightenment* as "man's emergence from his self-incurred immaturity." An enlightened person, he explained, should not allow traditions and institutions to do one's thinking. Instead, one should learn to think for oneself through the exercise of reason. By extension, Clark explained, humans no longer would turn to God to solve their problems but instead would use reason, science, and technology to take control of their destiny. Religious dogma would give way to scientific fact. Through rational planning, humans could reorganize society to create a better order, fight famine and disease, and raise the overall standard of living.

Viewing Clark's *Civilisation* several times, I decided that I wanted to be an enlightened, educated, modern man. I began reading many writers who were anticlerical if not antireligious in their views, and I soon followed suit, becoming a freethinker. I remember the Sunday morning when my mother climbed the stairs to my bedroom, knocked, and came in to ask if I was going to church. "Mom," I answered, "I don't believe in that stuff anymore." She immediately burst into tears. In retrospect I wish I had been more empathetic: this was a major blow for her. She and I never talked about my church non-attendance again.

I was a skeptical kid but far from cynical. In fact, I was enthusiastically idealistic and believed in the good of humanity. The crucifix came down from my bedroom wall and up went a black-and-white drawing, *Don Quixote de la Mancha*, by Pablo Picasso. The hit from the musical *Man of La Mancha* became my anthem—"To dream the impossible dream . . ."—and I went hunting for windmills.

After earning a BA at San Francisco State University, I was off on a new path as an atheist, a confirmed materialist (nothing exists except matter), and a devotee of reason. I refused to accept anything as true that couldn't be verified. Facts were all that mattered. The only faith I had was faith in us, humankind. I believed in the power of science and in the attainment of perfection through rational action. Had I lived at the end of the eighteenth century in France, I could have become a Jacobin and an ardent follower of the Cult of Reason—the Religion of Man. This was the atheistic creed established shortly after the 1789 revolution to replace Roman Catholicism. I was for *liberté, égalité, et fraternité*. I was for the perfection of humankind. I was for progress.

At the same time, I had come to believe that loving and wanting love were weaknesses to be overcome by force of will. Only weak-minded people needed love. You couldn't pull the wool over *my* eyes. Instead of becoming a lover or a saint, I was devoting my life to Truth. I would be a person of integrity. I aspired to be a tragic young man of principle.

After working for several years in the family's retail irrigation-parts business, I returned to San Francisco State to obtain an MA. I took several courses with Dr. Beverly Voloshin, one of which covered Restoration and eighteenth-century literary and philosophical texts. In that class, Voloshin assigned large portions of John Locke's 1690 *An Essay Concerning Human Understanding*. Never having read Locke before, I found him fascinating. Locke's *Essay* spoke to me, putting into words the principles of classical liberalism, which emphasized the rights of the individual—a universal rational human figure. These principles contributed to forming the basis of the rights tradition of autonomy that became an essential aspect of both Enlightenment and modern thinking. I became a Lockean fundamentalist, which is to say, a libertarian. Every individual, I was becoming convinced, could master his or her own destiny. If each person put his or her mind to it, anything was possible. Everyone could be independent and free, strong and self-reliant, standing like a saguaro cactus in the dry Arizona desert.

In Professor Voloshin's class I met Larry Buchalter. Larry was a person living with cerebral palsy who got around in a motorized chair, using a long white "unicorn" stick protruding from the front of his helmet to press buttons on a control panel in front of him. Thin, whiskered, wearing glasses, and probably in his late twenties, he was associated with the organization founded by disability rights pioneer Ed Roberts, Berkeley's Center for Independent Living, about which I knew nothing at the time. Larry rode BART from Berkeley, then transferred in San Francisco to a Muni street car, the M line, to reach the campus. In class he was extremely critical of Locke's philosophy, but I could never quite figure out what his objection to it was. One evening midway through the semester he called me. When I realized who it was I became petrified—it was as if Frankenstein's monster had dialed my number. He wanted to know if I would join him before class for coffee at the student union. Since we both were reading the same material, we could discuss it before heading into class. I didn't want to hang out with someone like that! I declined curtly and hung up. I couldn't have gotten off the phone any faster if something in my apartment had suddenly burst into flame.

Clio would crawl all over August's body before she started walking. He would lie prostrate on his Tumble Forms wedge, and from his expression I knew he liked having the rug rat crawl over his legs and back and head. It would excite him and make him smile and titter and kick his feet. He would even scream with delight. She called him Ba Ba.

After Clio began walking and as she grew older, August liked the way she would speak to him. Sometimes she would whisper into his ear. And sometimes she would put her arms around his head and give him kisses, and these actions would make him ecstatic.

"All happy families are alike; each unhappy family is unhappy in its own way"—that is the way Leo Tolstoy's novel *Anna Karenina* famously begins. As a family we weren't unhappy, at least with each other. But we were a family living life in its own way. Over time our world of personal interactions with others became confined to that of August's support system—therapists, doctors, nurses, coordinators, suppliers of adaptive equipment, and hired caregivers. As Roy Ellis notes in one of the items of his *30 Signs You May Have a Severely Disabled Child*: "You no longer have friends, just social workers and case managers."

Many friends dropped us because it was too hard to socialize with us and our challenging kid. And having a child like August made meeting new people hard. Finding friends became difficult because, to borrow wording from memoirist Vicki Forman, a "vague air of loneliness and desperation [began] surrounding us." No one else except for parents with kids like ours could really understand what we were going through. And usually these parents were too busy taking care of their own high-maintenance children to have much time for socializing. So we became isolated, a family marooned on a desert island. By virtue of there being no one else already present to vote us off, we were the survivors. We kept waiting to hear Jeff Probst of the reality TV program *Survivor* say, "The tribe has spoken. It's time for you to go." But there was no tribe, just us.

People who believe that a robust welfare system exists in a number of states—that is, one with adequate public assistance and support for families who have children such as ours—are likely to be surprised. Once in Florida, we discovered that there would be no public support whatsoever, just a waiting list. When we arrived in July 2001, the state's Agency for Persons with Disabilities (APD) put August's name on a waiting list to receive the Medicaid waiver (what he had had in California, the Medi-Cal waiver). Ahead of him were thousands of other children with severe impairments, and the wait for him to become eligible for desperately needed services was likely to extend a decade or longer. The estimate we received was that, at the earliest, he would start receiving the waiver in 2011. In the meantime, no government support services would be available. On account of their taxing and funding priorities, the state's governor and legislature had opted to throw families like ours under the bus. We were completely on our own.

"We're fucked!" This was how Ilene eloquently summed things up. And she was right. On account of August, we would be wiped out. What did this translate into? Just as friends, neighbors, and family had warned us, Ilene and I regularly had to forego pursuing lucrative career opportunities.

For Ilene, opening her own physical-therapy practice was out of the question—the amount of time required to successfully run a small business was not available because of August.

As for me, I was a scholar interrupted. Writing a book (something I needed to do to earn a promotion) while serving as the primary caregiver for a child with extraordinary needs was now an unrealistic expectation. To advance in most any career, be it in business, law, medicine, or academia, a person has to be willing and able to work sixty hours a week, sometimes more, at least at some points, and that would be impossible because of August. So we were both sidelined professionally. The problem boiled down to our inability to increase our earnings at the very time his already substantial medical expenses were growing even greater. We couldn't take on second jobs because his needs required us to be at home; we could barely work the jobs we already had. The increase in financial pressure while being unable to alleviate it was like discovering that the roof has burst into flame but the garden hose has no water to put it out. And so, even though we were both working full time, bankruptcy was in our future. Where before I had often just felt anxious, I now began to have panic attacks. What the hell were we going to do?

Whenever we mentioned to people the financial challenges associated with caring for August, something we tried to avoid doing, the believers in self-reliance would give advice that almost invariably started with the words "why don't you just." Why didn't we just get a second job, work more hours, organize a community 5K race, et cetera? From the outside, it must have all looked so easy. We would then have to explain that the amount of time required to care for August meant that no hours remained for implementing whatever it was they were suggesting, unless we were willing to leave August unattended at home for long periods of time. If we had done that, Florida's Department of Children and Families would have removed him from our care.

We had no family nearby to help, so Ilene and I had to hire young people and pay them out of pocket for respite care. We never wanted to hire help to care for our child, but we needed assistance in the evenings so that we could get our work done. Hiring helpers, however, meant that we were caught between Scylla and Charybdis: we couldn't afford to hire help, but we wouldn't be able to keep our jobs if we *didn't* hire help.

We also couldn't employ just anyone, such as a teenaged neighborhood babysitter, the usual recourse for the parents of typically developing children. A caregiver for August required a higher level of maturity and at least a month of intense training before Ilene and I could leave the person alone with him. A matter so seemingly simple as transferring him from his wheelchair to his bed could injure him. Similarly, feeding him had to be performed with patience, skill, and caution so that he would not choke on or aspirate his food or drink (and risk coming down with pneumonia).

I had good luck finding caregivers through the University of North Florida. Nursing, psychology, and community health majors worked out particularly well. On a few occasions, candidates for the job came to the house for an interview and were so visibly disturbed by August's circumstances that we never heard from them again. But on the whole, the women (only young women applied for the job) were wonderful people. Over the years, Ilene and I built a team of what the philosopher Eva Feder Kittay would term *dependency workers*. One member would drop out in order to move on to the next phase of her life, and a new recruit would come in to take her place. Some of them become permanent friends.

Families with children who are healthy and typically developing experience a privilege of which they are not aware. Those families with children who are disabled or suffer from serious health problems constantly live in dread, always waiting for the other shoe to drop. Parents can barely think beyond the here and now when they know that they are only one phone call away from a crisis that will engulf them, one involving not just health but also financial status. The repercussions of the latter could be extremely serious. Ilene and I didn't want to lose our house. Over the years we had to refinance it twice to cover August's medical expenses. Along the way, we were unable to put anything aside for retirement beyond my employer's defined contribution program.

Once Clio asked if we all could embark on a Disney-themed cruise. She wanted to escape being marooned on our August-centric island, to sail away. I understood how disappointing this must have been. Sisters and brothers of kids with severe impairments have it hard. She had to surrender a great deal on account of August. Ilene's and my minutes and hours with her brother took time away from her. Spontaneous jaunts for ice cream or pizza were rare because getting August ready even for a short trip took a lot of time. Snuggling on the couch watching television as a family occurred infrequently: August had needs. She never went to Disney World in Orlando, a mere two and a half hours away, at least not with her own family. We couldn't take August with us because he didn't travel easily, and we couldn't afford to hire someone to watch him while we were away for that long. The same went for going to the ocean. Even though it was only a thirty-minute drive to Atlantic Beach and an hour to the shore at Guana River State Park, we had to pay someone to watch him while we were away. There was nothing for him to do at the beach anyway, and rolling him in his wheelchair through the sand was impossible.

Often I sensed that the connection between my daughter and me had become strained. In the evenings when she was younger and had asked me to play with her, I had been forced to say no over and over because I'd had tasks to perform for her brother. After days of rejection, her defenses had gone up, and she had begun to ignore me, not deliberately but because she was too young to know how to put her hurt feelings into words.

But despite all of the deprivation, Clio never stopped loving August. She always remained proud of him, gave him hugs and kisses, sang to him, and exhibited toward him the most expansive, inclusive spirit. One day, years later, when she was barely twelve, she put on bright red lipstick and planted a lipstick kiss on his cheek. In a photo documenting this, he is grinning with the prize of love prominently displayed. Yet the picture is more complicated. We learned in later years that her response to the situation was extremely complex. Subtle psychological challenges arose with regard to having a sibling with so many impairments. Eventually she would have to work them out by meeting with a therapist.

Worry oppressed me almost night and day regarding what would happen to August after Ilene and I died. Clio would have to take over. And this greatly concerned me: why should her life be circumscribed by having to care for her sibling? She ought to be able to lead her own life. Because of the drama that would unfold someday—of Clio having to act as August's guardian—I began to think that it was absurd to build a society on the fantasy that everyone should depend solely on oneself. It was delusional to think that we could each make it on our own. Alexis de Tocqueville describes the shortcomings of individualism in writing about Americans in his 1835 *Democracy in America*:

> They owe nothing to any man, they expect nothing from any man; they acquire the habit of always considering themselves as standing alone, and they are apt to imagine that their whole destiny is in their own hands. Thus not only does democracy make every man forget his ancestors, but it hides his descendants and separates his contemporaries from him; it throws him back forever upon himself alone and threatens in the end to confine him entirely within the solitude of his own heart.

I became awakened to another viewpoint, that of a seventeenth-century alternative to John Locke. In "Meditation 17," John Donne writes, "No man is an island, entire of itself; every man is a piece of the continent, a part of the main." Donne's meditation gave me the sailing directions I needed for departing our island and traveling to the mainland. So we left our small island, the rock of independence, and embarked for the continent, the land of interdependence.

IV

A SENTENCE FROM A 1715 ISSUE OF *TOWN TALK*, A
London periodical, summed up our sentiment: "It is a wise
dictate of Nature that we love those children dearest whom
she presents to our care with the most infirmities." At the
beginning of each day I would pass through the laundry
room and open the white door to August's sleeping quarters,
a small room at the back of the Capote house. August's little
elfin grot was a space about the size of a one-car garage.
The door, baseboards, and two window frames were painted
white, and the four walls were a baby blue shade that Benja-
min Moore called Windmill Wings.

Every morning during early March, at a few minutes before seven o'clock, a horizontal ray would shoot through an
east-facing window and flare diagonally through the cham-
ber. For the time it takes a matchstick to burn, it would il-
luminate the room's west wall. The signature of this beam
would be no larger than a quarter, and it would land just
above and to the right of the headboard of August's electric hospital bed. Sherwin-Williams would label this hue
Laughing Orange. This spot on the wall was the sunrise and
the cue for my aubade to August. "Wakee! Wakee!" I would
call out as I came through his white door. I would touch his
shoulder and pull down his covers and then raise the blinds.

Light of the new day—the good-morrow—would stream in. August would open his eyes, stretch, coo, grin, and kick at the bed covers with glee.

From outside would come the resolute tapping of woodpeckers and the morning calls of gray catbirds, brown thrashers, and mockingbirds, all singing their hearts out. This was our parliament of fowls. For the most part I didn't know which birdsong was which; I just knew that these were common birds in our area. I would join in with my own morning call, the "Good Morning Song." As I began to sing sweetly, August would brighten further and wait for what he knew was coming. When I came to the penultimate line, I would screech it out in an exaggerated, creaky voice like that of Margaret Hamilton's Wicked Witch of the West from *The Wizard of Oz*: "Good morning to the bunny rabbit named August!" Hearing this, August would kick and squeal.

I then would get him ready for the day by changing his diaper, bathing him, brushing his teeth, and dressing him. I loved his warmth, his body heat, as I tended to him. Every day, I would silently note that he had a belly button like a jellyroll.

August had an exquisiteness about him. At birth his eyes had been green, but over time they softened to hazel. He had a winsome, well-shaped face with high cheekbones. His hair when he was born had been red, but over time it settled into light brown and became soft, thick, and fluffy.

In the mornings August's vision was at its best because he was rested. His eyes would roam about, scanning and visually taking in the room and me as I went about assembling everything to prepare him for the day—washcloths, toothbrush, fresh diaper, and clothes. August could see very little, and the condition of his sight was officially labeled *cortical visual impairment,* or CVI. With CVI, his optic nerves worked perfectly well, but because he had suffered brain damage, the cortex had great difficulty making sense of the data it was receiving from these nerves. Therapists told us that sight for August was like looking through many sheets of cellophane. If he had experienced a good night's sleep, he might be able to pick out colors and shapes, but little more. Whether he could make sense of them was another matter. The only major sign from August's appearance that he had suffered a significant brain injury was the way his eyes moved. His eyeballs shifted in slow motion. His saccades—or fast movements of the eye (something we all have but don't notice in one another because the movements are so rapid)—were poor, owing to the damage to his cortex. And so, with slowed saccades, August swept his visual field.

His best vision was peripheral: he could take things in with brief sideward glances. Consequently, when he appeared to be looking directly at me, I knew that he actually wasn't seeing me at all. But if his body was turned ninety degrees away from me, as when he sat sideways on my lap, and he shifted his head slightly toward my face and gave me a quick glance out of the corner of his eye, I knew that he was briefly taking me into his field of vision. On these occasions he'd shoot me an infatuating little smile.

Sometimes he would stick his finger into his eye socket, and a vision specialist we consulted speculated that he was doing this to stimulate light sensation. I wouldn't let him do this though—not because he was going to gouge an eye out, but because I didn't want him to damage the cornea. "Don't do that," I'd say each time as I removed his finger from his eye. "You're not Oedipus."

Back in 1999, when we were still in San Francisco, one of August's therapists—a friend—had written in a report that on account of August's brain injury he had increased tone in all of his limbs, but decreased tone in his neck and trunk muscles. This combination brought about "severely limited active volitional movement." Seven years later, her assessment remained accurate. He couldn't move his limbs, except for his legs, which he was able to kick, and his left arm, which he could flail. Moreover, August never improved intellectually. His developmental gap continued to widen. He was only going to make it to about a one-year-old level by the time he was an adult, if that. He was like a baby who kept growing bigger and bigger without any increase in skills and abilities.

The therapist producing this report was describing him from the vantage point of science, and what she wrote was accurate, as far as it went. "Profoundly retarded" was the label that another professional used regarding him. "Retarded" is the condition that society, in the words of English professor Janet Lyon of Penn State (and mother of Jamie Bérubé), assumes to be "the lowest rung" of humanity.

When we brought August home from Loma Prieta years earlier, we had entertained high hopes regarding recovery from the brain injury. Dr. Anderson at the family consult seven days after the birth had been encouraging, saying that August would probably meet his milestones. But Ilene and I had never encountered a child who was in this state. I myself was unaware that such children even existed. Had we parented August with only the doctors' and therapists' descriptions to go by, we might have thrown up our hands in despair. But we knew that August was more than a smoking heap of terrible conditions. Because we saw that he was a happy and lively being, we didn't let the medical terminology or bioethical stereotypes govern our thinking about him.

We turned instead to the imagination, because that is what makes us human. Life without it would be life in a dungeon. If knowledge is power, imagination is destiny. A scientific, empirical description turned August into human rubble, a car wreck that had happened in the delivery suite, but imagination allowed us to move the medical diagnoses to the curb so we could reach our boy. In our minds' eye he wasn't all that different. He was August, just one member of a quirky family.

August had become a devotee of the senses. Cultivating whatever gave pleasure became the chief business of his life. He did not know of any occupation that was more important, and he was extravagantly fond of good food. August would bite his left hand when he was hungry, and that's when I knew it was time for him to eat. Fearing reflux, San Francisco therapists had directed us to only give him Pedia-Sure. The therapists at the DLC Nurse & Learn helped him transition to eating bananas, sweet potatoes, and other soft dishes. He could consume food with textures, food finely chopped but not pureed.

Each portion of food and sip of liquid had to be hand-delivered to his mouth, like feeding a baby bird. Because he could not see, we cued each bite or sip with the clearly articulated words "food!" "milk!" or "water!" whereupon his little pink mouth would pop open. We would bring the spoon or cup to his mouth, he would take in the food or drink, and then we would linger, sometimes for up to thirty seconds, allowing him to swallow before offering him more. We could not hurry; if we did, he might aspirate what was in his mouth.

August was not a fussy eater. Banana mashed with a crushed graham cracker became one of his preferred mid-afternoon snacks. For dinners, sweet potatoes with a pat of butter and a dab of maple syrup proved a preferred dish. To vary his diet, we produced thick, semi-pureed concoctions of enchiladas, lasagna, or chicken mixed with carrots, broccoli, and broth. Tasty food made him utter a soft, murmuring coo. Eventually, for dessert, we were able to feed him a cookie.

His sense of smell was sharp too. He loved the aroma of coffee, and whenever I placed a steaming cup beneath his nostrils, his smile broadened.

He loved ice cream the most. Whenever he took in the first bite, his face would scrunch up into a deep pucker, seemingly an agonized response to the coldness. Next, he would work it around his mouth with his tongue, and finally he would swallow it. We could practically see his brain freeze. You might conclude from his initial pained expression that he wouldn't want more, that eating ice cream was too excruciating. A couple of seconds would elapse, though, and then—without anyone having to say the cue word "food!"—his mouth would open for more. So entertaining a spectacle was this that it became performance art.

He delighted in parties. During Clio's annual birthday celebrations, with her young friends shouting, laughing, and playing games, he remained silent in his wheelchair, perplexed by the sounds. But then, after the party had wound down and the children had gone home, he would begin to bellow loudly, as though he had finally figured out the meaning of the voices. Now, belatedly, he had something to contribute. Or perhaps he wanted her friends to come back.

Because August was not able to walk, he had little of what is called vestibular stimulation. This is the process of sending specific electric messages to a nerve in the ear. When he was much younger and smaller, I had been able to lay him over my shoulder and hop up and down, either on pavement or in the swimming pool at the Jewish Community Association. When he became bigger and heavier, therapy balls substituted. After laying him face down on a very large one, I would roll him rapidly back and forth or bounce him up and down in place, and these motions would make him shriek with pleasure. As he grew, Ilene and I had to keep moving up to larger and larger therapy balls. When he had grown so much that no ball was large enough, we had to go big or go home by ordering the most massive such thing in the catalog, the blue peanut. The blue peanut was a two-and-a-half-foot-high oblong "ball" indented in the middle, and it was huge—it took up a lot of the playroom. We were able to plant August face-down in the peanut's middle, and he would become ecstatic whenever we gave him a workout. When I would make him go really, really fast, backward and forward, he'd screech.

When I went running, August would join me—by sitting in a blue, supersized "special needs" Baby Jogger, the largest the company made. I remember one mid-afternoon, when he was nine years old, in 2008. The humidity being relatively mild and the temperature not overly hot, I judged it would be a good time to put him in the Jogger. It was overcast when we set off, but not, I thought, so dark that a storm threatened. Very often, summer afternoons all over Florida are positively gothic, with lightning, thunder, and dense tropical rain. The state also is the lightning-strike capital of the world.

Running, I pushed August north on San Jose Boulevard, past the wide expanse of the Duck Pond, the one-story red-

brick schoolhouse (and the lush green meadow surrounding it), and the eastern tip of primordial Craig Creek. We
crossed Hendricks Avenue at the traffic light and headed
toward the eastern edge of the San Marco neighborhood,
where a rail line intersects St. Augustine Road. There, on
the south side of the tracks, and three quarters of a mile
east of Craig Creek, is a three-acre tree-shaded graveyard, a
secluded spot where the rude forefathers of our hamlet sleep.
Dating back to the 1840s, the Philips–Craig Swamp Cemetery was, by 2008, forgotten and overgrown. It was tidied
up in 2017, but when August and I went there, it was wild.
Inside the gates, he and I made our way.

This was my favorite place in Jacksonville. Ironically, it
was this graveyard where the city first came alive for me.
Ragged, fully grown trident maples and moss-draped live
oaks populated the grounds. A tall scruffy cypress stood by
the tracks, and a low ancient palm tree squatted in the center. Toward the back, a large tree had fallen in a long ago
hurricane, and now its rotting trunk lay lengthwise along
the ground like a low, cylindrical wall. No lawn surrounded
the mossy tombstones, just weeds, and I maneuvered as well
as I could over the uneven surface, an infielder's nightmare.
The turf heaved throughout these burial grounds with tree
roots and branches and moldering graves. Both Union and
Confederate dead had been interred there. The Jogger ca-
reened around them as we dodged frail memorials and
toppled monuments. Pushing August over the soil's jagged
plane jostled and jarred him, and the rough motion made
him squeal. The more rugged the terrain, the bumpier the
ride, and the more it jolted him, the more he shouted for joy.

I'd been so caught up in his excitement that I hadn't noticed the storm clouds moving in. Leaving the cemetery, we

smelled the rain before we felt it. August delighted in the droplets that began landing on his bare arms and legs, and he made appreciative sounds. The Jogger's awning protected his head. As we reached Hendricks Avenue and headed south, I was grateful that it was only sprinkling. We crossed Hendricks at the light and skirted the eastern tip of Craig Creek, but then, heading south on our home street, the storm exploded. Instantly I was soaked. Powerful winds began to blow, and I wondered if a tornado was forming. Lightning and thunder commenced, with forked incandescent streaks rippling the sky. The interval between the flashes of light and the thunderclaps became about a second. We still had half a mile to go. August sat silently, stunned by the sublimity. The torrent slapped my face, and the world withdrew into gray: the red schoolhouse and green meadow vanished. The broad surface of the Duck Pond, pelted with rain, shimmered. I dashed August up our long driveway to the protection of a carport. After whisking him out of the Jogger, I carried him into the house, laid him on his big changing table, removed his drenched clothes, toweled him off, and dressed him in dry clothes. All the while he beamed and cooed, invigorated by our big adventure in the wild.

Every night after I had dressed him in his pajamas, brushed his teeth, and placed him on the sheets, it was time for a lullaby, "Returning," by Ajamu Mutima. Mutima is a master of the kora, the twenty-one-string West African harp-lute. I would turn on the CD player, turn off the overhead light, snap on his little night lamp, and make certain the sound monitor was on.

Some people may suppose that, because my son's character was as airy as a dandelion gone to seed, I never got a chance to know my boy. In the darkness, as Mutima softly played the kora, I would lean over the bed railing so that my face would be very close to his head. As the moon waxed and waned, rose and fell, pulling the tides in ebbs and flows all around the planet, I would think of two lines from a John Donne poem: "For love, all love of other sights controls, / And makes one little room an everywhere."

Our communication was closest at bedtime, when we entered our separate reality most profoundly, and I would speak nonsense sounds into his ear, telling him wordlessly that I loved him, and he in his own singular way would tell me the same thing. His response would be to incline his face toward mine and grin, and sometimes he would cackle with glee, the laugh of Medusa. I would whisper, "My darling boy, my moon and stars," and he—a little chucklehead—would giggle. Into the night August and I had many a deep conversation, ones as sweet as being put under with Propofol.

After August's birth, I didn't find many role models of fathers taking care of disabled children. I read quite a bit of helpful material by women on mothering such children, with Eva Feder Kittay's 1999 book *Love's Labor* being particularly helpful. Traditionally the caregiver role has almost always fallen on women; it is only recently that men have begun assuming it. When men become active caregivers, their work is regarded as unusual and therefore heroic. By contrast, women become remarkable only when they refuse, whereupon they become the butt of criticism. This difference reminds us of our society's profound and persistent patriarchal bias.

What sources of inspiration would I need to help me learn how to play this new role? I was looking for examples of men who had taken up this challenge. I came across Dick Hoyt, the father of Rick, who lives with cerebral palsy. Years later I would read Dick's 2010 memoir, *Devoted: The Story of a Father's Love for His Son*. Together they had taken part in more than thirty Boston Marathons, with Dick pushing Rick in a modified wheelchair.

Reading opened me to other models. In the decade or more following August's birth, I found notable books by men caring for children with impairments, including Michael Bérubé's *Life as We Know It* and his follow-up, *Life as Jamie Knows It*, Ralph Savarese's *Reasonable People*, Gary Dietz's *Dads of Disability*, George Estreich's *The Shape of an Eye*, Kirby Wilkins's *Life with Jake*, Diogo Mainardi's *The Fall*, and Ian Brown's *The Boy in the Moon*.

This isn't to say that there aren't good caregiver accounts by women. Many exist, too many to name. A list would have to include Vicki Forman's *This Lovely Life*, Glenda Prins's *Lessons from Katherine*, Emily Rapp's *The Still Point of the Turning World*, and Rachel Adams's *Raising Henry*. I was learning a lot about disability, and, in turn, I was discovering my own disablism—prejudice against disabled people.

People first hearing about our boy immediately assume heartbreak. They do so because they have in their minds a single story about disabled children and the families that raise them—the tragic story. "Society sees disability as the worst thing that can happen," says scholar and disability rights activist Tom Shakespeare. "It's one thing that can happen, but not the worst."

As August grew older, we grew too. We were learning the difference between disability and impairment. As disability studies scholar Lennard Davis puts it in *Bending Over Backwards*, impairment "is the physical fact of lacking an arm or a leg. Disability is the social process that turns an impairment into a negative by creating barriers to access." A building without a ramp or an elevator turns mobility impairment into a disability. The overarching idea behind this insight is one that Davis expresses in another context: "The 'problem' is not the person with disabilities; the problem is the way that normalcy is constructed to create the 'problem' of the disabled person." Davis's distinction—known as the *social model* of disability—made sense to me because it usefully differentiated impairment from disability. It was also tactically effective when disability rights activists campaigned for greater access and accommodation. We didn't know it at the time, but back in early 2000, when we sued the Child Care Center at Presidio Heights to get August reinstated, it was this very distinction between disability and impairment that was at stake.

At the beginning I had just assumed that the experience of raising a disabled child was supposed to be anything but beautiful. But my mind was changed by the late Harriet McBryde Johnson, whose article "Unspeakable Conversations" came out in a February 2003 Sunday edition of the *New York Times*. A disability-rights campaigner and a woman living with a muscle-wasting disease, Johnson had visited Peter Singer in his Princeton University classroom, doing so on behalf of Not Dead Yet, a group opposing child euthanasia and physician-assisted suicide. She was gutsy, diplomatically confrontational, and smart in her exchange with the man the *Encyclopædia Britannica* calls "one of the world's most widely recognized public intellectuals."

Because she was born with a congenital impairment, Johnson could have been one of the infants whose life was terminated shortly after birth. Consequently, she was an ideal person to debate Singer. She was also an atheist, so he couldn't accuse her of arguing against his position on religious grounds, which he dismissed outright. People of faith who opposed his beliefs were a dime a dozen. It was precisely because she was both an atheist and someone living with a significant congenital defect that Singer was somewhat thrown back on his heels.

Singer advocates in favor of decriminalizing child euthanasia, and he lays out this view in various writings, including his 1988 book *Should the Baby Live? The Problem of Handicapped Infants* (coauthored with Helga Kuhse). He believes that new parents ought to be given the option of deciding whether or not to keep their impaired (or even their unimpaired) newborns alive. These parents should have an assessment period of up to twenty-one days after the birth to choose whether or not they want to take the baby home or to allow doctors to terminate his or her life. Singer does not address the issue of what to do in the case of a myriad of serious medical conditions that do not present in the first twenty-one days of life. With regard to an infant born with an apparent problem, parents would be able to reject that infant so that they could try again, to see if they could conceive a "better" baby. The core of his proposal—putting an end to suffering and eliminating waste—aligned with the Enlightenment goal of improving quality of life by judiciously organizing human affairs.

Singer is a *preference utilitarian*, meaning his stance is rooted in a strain of utilitarianism that stems from Jeremy Bentham and Bentham's student John Stuart Mill, both of whom contend that what should be considered "the good" is whatever benefits the greatest number of people. Along utilitarian lines Singer maintains that society has an interest in conserving its limited resources, and so cost of treatment and care should be a major consideration in public policy decisions. Society, he argues, should allocate its assets for the maximum benefit of its members who are physically and mentally able and not expend them on those born with serious defects.

Singer believes that legalizing child euthanasia would promote "the good" of couples by expanding the range of choices available to them when it comes to forming the kinds of families they want to have. When explaining the reasons why new parents would want to terminate their infants' lives, Singer often brings up the example of infants born with Down syndrome. Down syndrome is the test case he frequently returns to, and here he seems to be working from an old paradigm. But conditions have changed, as M. Lynn Rose makes clear in *The Routledge History of Disability*:

> Only a generation or two ago, babies born with Down Syndrome were not expected to live very long, and so they were routinely placed in institutions, where, denied the basic comforts of childhood, they didn't live very long. Since the early 1980s, the life expectancy of people with Down Syndrome has doubled, not because of some breakthrough medical advance, but because of higher expectations coupled with appropriate resources.

Our understanding of Down syndrome and what is possible for those born with it has changed dramatically just in the course of a few decades. Yet Singer continues to espouse his ideas in his lectures and more recent writings.

While Singer most frequently invokes babies born with Down syndrome to make his case, the lives of those born with other impairments such as fragile X syndrome, spina bifida, cystic fibrosis, cerebral palsy, profound cognitive impairment, and so forth also would be subject to the parents' preference if he had his way. In fact, depending on the decision of the parents, *any* baby—regardless of health status or impairment—could be subject to having his or her life ended. It would be as though legal abortion would extend into the fourth trimester. Still, babies with birth defects are his main focus because infants with impairments, he believes, will be inherently worse off than those unimpaired. Their lives will be permeated with suffering and therefore will not be worth living. He is one of the many philosophers who are openly skeptical of the idea that disability is not intrinsically suboptimal.

Singer's philosophy fits in well with a culture that equates *personhood* with autonomy, self-reliance, and individuality. A *person*, according to Singer, is an entity that has consciousness of itself in relation to time and space and is aware that it is going to die. As for the supposed right of infants to life, he maintains that they are not legally persons (fully human) with rights. A baby lacks this awareness and so is not yet a person with a right to life. Regarding infants with impairments, because they are not yet persons, and because they supposedly will be miserable when they grow older, it would not be wrong—but in fact would be humane—to end their lives at the beginning. He writes in his 1979 book *Practical Ethics*:

> That a being is a human being . . . is not relevant to the wrongness of killing it; it is, rather, characteristics like rationality, autonomy and self-consciousness that make a difference. Defective infants lack these characteristics.

Killing them, therefore, cannot be equated with killing normal human beings, or any other self-conscious beings. This conclusion is not limited to infants who, because of irreversible mental retardation will never be rational, self-conscious beings. . . . Some doctors closely connected with children suffering from severe spina bifida believe that the lives of some of these children are so miserable that it is wrong to resort to surgery to keep them alive. . . . If this is correct, utilitarian principles suggest that it is right to kill such children.

Singer is hardly alone in advocating child euthanasia. Throughout his life Joseph Fletcher, a pioneer in the field of bioethics, was a leading proponent of it. And other bioethicists, such as Jeff McMahan and Jacob Appel, have presented similar ideas. Many bioethicists, in fact, see the reasonableness of child euthanasia.

Child euthanasia is not a new concept. It became popular during the eugenics era—the first four decades of the twentieth century in Britain and the United States. (Eugenics was the belief that various peoples and nations and even the whole human race could be improved through better breeding, somewhat like creating thoroughbred lines of dogs and horses.) In 1915 the chief surgeon of a major Chicago hospital, Harry Haiselden, on becoming involved in the Baby Bollinger case, campaigned vigorously for child euthanasia. He convinced the parents of the infant John Bollinger that the best option for society and for John, their child born with physical anomalies, was to let him die, claiming that the child would live a miserable life and drain public resources. In the face of public protest, Haiselden argued at a press conference that "mercy killing" for such a child was more humane than letting him live. Many prominent figures defended him, among them Helen Keller and Clarence Darrow.

In 1917 Haiselden wrote and starred in the movie *The Black Stork*, a polemical film supporting "lethal eugenics"—the third stage in eugenic thought—the active taking of life, euthanasia. The first two stages did not involve deliberate killing. The first entailed encouraging only the "fittest" individuals to form into couples and procreate. The second involved the forced sterilization of mental or physical "defectives," and a number of states executed this practice; the US Supreme Court ruled the procedure constitutional in its 1927 decision *Buck v. Bell* on the grounds that eugenic sterilization served the good of the state. (California, by the way, outpaced all other states in the number of people its officials ordered sterilized.) Haiselden was an early supporter of a third stage, the taking of life, the kind of thing Singer now advocates. By the time of *Buck v. Bell*, the public was becoming more and more accepting of all three stages, including Haiselden's lethal eugenics. While support was widespread, it also was quiet. It wasn't until the liberation of the Nazi death camps in 1945 that support evaporated. Interest in "neo-eugenics" is now rising under the auspices of the Human Genome Project, and genetic engineering is gaining traction with the public.

When Harriet Johnson debated Singer in his Princeton classroom before his philosophy students, in effect she had to argue in favor of her own existence. With regard to this encounter, she later wrote, "I am reminded of a young woman I knew as a child, lying on a couch, brain-damaged, apparently unresponsive, and deeply beloved—freakishly perhaps but genuinely so—living proof of one family's no-matter-what commitment." During the interchange, she had brought this young woman up, and Singer had responded by asking, "Don't you think continuing to take care of that individual would be a bit—weird?"

"Done right," Johnson replied, "it could be profoundly beautiful."

When I read this in her *New York Times* account, I was stunned. It had never crossed my mind in quite that way. It could be beautiful? The rational thing to do would have been to smother the person with a pillow. Johnson had given me a vision. The question then became how, as a dad, I was to do this. I now desired not only to be August's champion and friend but also to perform the whole affair with a sense of aesthetics, as the masterwork of my life. If I couldn't be a great scholar, at least I could be a great father to August. I would make caring for him as profoundly beautiful as I could.

V

MY SON DID NOT BREAK MY BELIEF IN FACTS AND reason so much as end my blind faith in them. It was not that they didn't matter anymore but that they were not *all* that mattered. Love was something else. It was a separate reality. If he were alive to observe and comment on my life with August, the Romantic poet Samuel Taylor Coleridge would in all likelihood judge me, as he did the figure of Betty Foy in a poem titled "The Idiot Boy" by his friend and poetic collaborator William Wordsworth, an "impersonation of an instinct abandoned by judgment." This had once made sense to me, but by this later point I had begun to understand life differently and so would have retorted, "What is love if not 'instinct abandoned by judgment'?" Not understanding Betty Foy's motivation, her profound parental love for her child, was a failure of imagination on Coleridge's part. Maybe my behavior was evidence of unredeemable stupidity. There was a time when I would have thought so. I once believed that loving and wanting love were weaknesses to be overcome, that only weak-minded people needed love. By now, though, I had come around to a different way of thinking, that it is not the unexamined life that is not worth living but the life without love.

August's skills actually increased, albeit incrementally and at a glacial pace. Advancements came so slowly that they snuck up on us. In the early spring of 2006, when August was almost seven, the Mt. Herman occupational therapists began getting him used to walking in a Rifton gait trainer. Mt. Herman's corridors were solidly parked on both sides with Riftons the way cars line the curbs in San Francisco. These were pieces of equipment similar to the Mulholland stander of August's toddler days. The Rifton too is a standing device, but it differs from the Mulholland in that it allows the person in it to plant his or her feet firmly on the ground. A person in a Rifton can self-propel forward—in others words, can walk.

At first August furiously resisted. For six months he propelled himself up and down the corridors taking big angry strides and crying loudly. Eventually, though, he adjusted and grew to love being in it. The first time I saw him taking steps and smiling I burst into tears. I decided right then that we had to have a Rifton at home for him to walk up and down our long driveway. When I discovered that the cost of one was the equivalent of two mortgage payments and that insurance wouldn't cover the expense, Ilene and I decided to dip further into what was left of our savings.

When we rolled August in his wheelchair through the kitchen door out into the open air, he became hysterical with joy. Down the ramp we rumbled, through the carport, and out onto the driveway. When he was relatively small, the caregivers—university students Ilene and I had begun to hire—were able to transfer him into the Rifton on their own, scooping him up from his wheelchair, carrying him to it, and dropping his legs down into the center of the device.

As he grew older, bigger, and heavier, they more and more needed my assistance. When the preparations were complete, we released the brakes. Our driveway was long and paved, and he often tooled up and down the full length of it. The spasticity of his cerebral palsy made his leg and head thrusts wildly ungainly. His was a jerky, staccato motion. One time he marched the length of the driveway and, because I wasn't paying attention, he almost entered the street. I sprinted down and caught him just in time. Up until his eleventh year he strode up and down the driveway like a tin soldier needing oil.

I believed that August was living a satisfying life. How, though, could I have speculated about his thoughts, feelings, and level of life satisfaction? How did I avoid being presumptuous? How dare I speak for a nonverbal person? It is around this last issue that I began to detect a disconnect between the goals of the disability rights movement and the needs of our son. The movement promoted the emancipatory project of independence and self-determination for disabled people. The individuals spearheading this social justice campaign were primarily people with able minds living with mobility or sensory impairments. The possibility of living and working independently in the community would indeed be realizable for them, if only society would lower its barriers to access. In this, the movement was attempting to implement for the disabled community an Enlightenment legacy: the Lockean, libertarian dream of freedom.

But this dream would never be feasible for August. He epitomized an Enlightenment paradox: he had been raised like Lazarus from the dead by medical intervention, but he was profoundly cognitively impaired on account of that intervention and so was unable to live independently. He would forever require assistance with hygiene, feeding, bathing, dressing, and daily recreational activities. Most importantly, he would always need someone to speak for him. Over time, I found that many disability rights activists and scholars could not imagine him—could not (or did not want to) conceive of a person with such an extreme level of deficit. Moreover, on a few occasions when I spoke for August, I was answered with hostility. The movement had a hard time figuring out what to do with disabled people's parents, whom it regarded with suspicion (often rightly so). The implication was that I needed to get out of my son's way. I was blocking his development, silencing his aspirations, and thwarting his self-realization.

As a disabled person, August occupied an uneasy place in the movement. In fact, he was an outlier, a marginalized figure even among the disabled. Because he couldn't keep up with their drive for independent living, and because he could not speak for himself, they had to leave him behind. While I understood and accepted the rationale for why this had to be so, the realization that even this movement was leaving our son behind brought on a gloomy mood.

Still, I did not become disillusioned with the movement. Some in it did in fact embrace and champion people like August, chief among them Harriet McBryde Johnson. In her 2005 *Slate* piece defending the right of Terri Schiavo to remain alive ("Not Dead at All"), she articulated an objective for which I could strive on August's behalf, one far more humble than that for which the movement generally was aiming. Her vision for people like him was that of a dignified and inclusive existence. Rather than independent living and the slogan "Nothing about us without us," the appropriate social and political principle to campaign for in August's interest would be that in which his dignity as a human being and his right to remain alive would be recognized.

The question of care also was controversial in the disability rights movement. The word *care* was to be resisted, and the activity of caregiving was not infrequently demonized. Of course, care has been a site of oppression for disabled people. People have died on account of care done poorly. But August would have died without care. Care sometimes is necessary to insure the survival of vulnerable people. For good reason, care was a contested issue, but I sometimes lost patience with people who casually dismissed its necessity.

In my case with August, the issue of care needed to be reformulated. What required consideration was a mutually beneficial ethics of care. My role as caregiver, the one I crafted for myself, was that of not adhering to a so-called custodial care model, the one followed in institutions and implemented by their minimum-wage attendants, but of practicing caring labor. The concept of caring labor was one I picked up from reading a 2002 article by Pamela Cushing and Tanya Lewis published in the journal *Hypatia*. Caring labor became my theme. What did this entail? I made it a point to learn and recognize August's little ways. These were his subtle expressions—the twitch of his lips, the shift of an eyebrow. He grimaced; he grinned. He fussed; he laughed. He let me know what he wanted or needed. Putting his hand in his mouth in a particular way indicated he was hungry, and he made a certain sound when he wanted to go to bed.

Attentive to his cues, I viewed the connection we had as one of mutuality. Our lives together were characterized neither by his dependence on me nor by my surrender of independence to him. Rather, we lived in a world of interdependence. We depended upon one another in radically different ways. Caregiving was not an expression of selfless idealism on my part. I did not do it because I was charitable, altruistic, saintly, or stalwart. In truth, I needed him as much as he did me. If I didn't love him, all of this effort would have been a grudging sacrifice. But he made me happy, and so, in our peculiar way, we split everything down the middle.

Within our household, August seemed normal enough, but whenever out in public we were constantly reminded how unusual he appeared to other people. What had become ordinary for us at home triggered awkward, exaggerated, and even pained visceral reactions outside of it. He shocked people. Although he was still a little boy, and a handsome little boy at that, they responded as though he were a monster. They either gawked or looked away blatantly, as if a glance at him would freeze them in their tracks.

August's disabilities offered ample opportunity for public interpretation. Occasionally someone would come up to us and say that we were blessed. I suppose it could have been worse: they might have told us that we were cursed. People would give unsolicited advice and offer banal inspirational sayings such as "Everything happens for a reason." Some would extend hollow encouragement, often of a religious nature, such as "God chose well when he made you his parents" and "God doesn't send you anything you can't handle" and "This is a part of God's plan." The worst was the one Erma Bombeck coined in 1980: "God gives special kids to special parents." According to *Wikipedia*, Bombeck was a humorist.

And there were people who would say, "I can't imagine what you're going through." The people who said this divided into two camps. For the vast majority, it was a genuine expression of compassion. When they told us, "I can't imagine . . .," they were speaking ironically, saying the opposite of what they meant. They actually *could* imagine enough of our situation to recognize that it was a difficult one, and so they were signaling their support and wishing us well. But a few would say "I can't imagine . . ." to imply their superiority. This usually came from well-educated people implying that we should have aborted. Their veiled message was, "Weren't you smart enough to get tested?" They were too intelligent to allow something similar to happen to themselves. They were unaware, of course, that the warning signs hadn't appeared until two days after August's due date, and, the last time I'd checked, abortions were still illegal in the fourth trimester.

Privately, I would treat August with the dignity he deserved, and publicly I would demand that others do the same. This policy came down to even the smallest things. For example, I always adhered to a strict code, one stipulating that I would never say anything to or about him that I would not want him to understand, were he able to do so. Even if I could make people laugh, I wasn't going to do it at his expense. Some fathers adopt a different approach. In his book *Where We Going, Daddy?* Jean-Louis Fournier frequently makes jokes at the expense of his two severely impaired children, Mathieu and Thomas. This book won a literary prize in France, and an NPR critic praised Fournier for writing "honestly and admirably about something off-limits to most everyone else." Suffice it to say that I find making fun of one's disabled children for the public's amusement neither honest nor admirable. Still, I don't want to come down too hard on Fournier: having such children is not easy.

My own brand of irreverence attempted to rope August into the joke. One morning in the spring of 2006 I was wheeling him around San Marco Square by the fountain and the three big bronze lions. A well-dressed middle-aged woman came up to us and showed great interest, as people on occasion did.

"Who is this?" she said enthusiastically as she bent down to get a closer look.

And I replied, assuming a God-like tone, "This is my beloved son in whom I am well pleased."

In June 2005, August was suddenly and unexpectedly granted the Medicaid waiver. For many months Ilene had petitioned our elected representatives for help, attempting through letters, emails, and phone calls to find an official to pay heed to our situation. Finally a woman working in the office of State Senator Stephen Wise called back and, with the senator's help, she pulled strings with Florida's Agency for Persons with Disabilities and got our son off the wait list. After being granted the waiver, he became eligible for what in Florida is called Consumer Directed Care Plus, or CDC+. With it, we found that our out-of-pocket expenses remained exorbitant but that our financial hemorrhaging stopped. Subsequently, whenever Ilene contacted a state agency representative by phone, it was not uncommon for her to be addressed condescendingly. This was not true of the support coordinators and service providers interacting directly with families like ours at the local level; people who worked with us face-to-face generally were helpful. But the people in Tallahassee, the state capital, treated us differently. To them, Ilene was a mother whose child had a disability that must have stemmed from drug or alcohol abuse or some other bad behavior during pregnancy. Because of this supposed moral failing, she must have done something to cause August to be the way he was. His impairments provided them with an opportunity for mother shaming. To them, these problems disclosed her lack of love, willpower, and maternal dedication. Consequently, when she spoke with them, they always seemed to be on the verge of asking, "Have you stopped smoking crack yet?" Our encounters with the Tallahassee office of the Agency for Persons with Disabilities reminded me of a line from Aleksandr Solzhenitsyn's *One Day in the Life of Ivan Denisovich:* "How can you expect a man who is warm to understand one who is cold?"

Then, in April 2009, everything in our family's domestic arrangement changed. August had grown big and heavy, and Ilene suffered a herniated disc in her neck brought about by lifting him. For several months she was laid up in bed. An articulating titanium disc had to be inserted into her vertebral column at neck level to replace the deteriorated one. Afterward, her doctor told her to not lift any weight beyond fifty pounds. Because August by then weighed more than seventy pounds, I had to assume all of his caregiving—his daily dressing and hygiene and transportation to all doctor and therapy appointments, to his school each morning, and from the after-school facility each afternoon.

After Ilene went back to work full time, she took on the responsibility of making all the phone calls for August's care and sorting through the mountains of bills. August generated a lot of paperwork from pharmacies, doctors, therapists, and our insurance company. She spent many hours on hold listening to canned music while waiting to speak with a representative of one company or another about problems with a medical bill, a medication error, or an insurance company claim. Our insurance company—no fly-by-night discount operation but supposedly one of Florida's best—frequently denied our claims. In fact, we constantly struggled with systematic denial. There was so much that insurance just wouldn't cover. Ilene would then have to spend hours appealing the decision, sometimes successfully, sometimes not. Occasionally the device, procedure, or medical office visit for which the claim was denied was explicitly covered according to the terms of our policy. We could have sued, but attorneys taking such cases require a retainer of $20,000 to $30,000.

The additional responsibilities at home now subtracted a sizable number of hours out of my workday. Because I was the only person in the household able to lift August, I could not be away from home for more than eight hours at a time, if even for that. Every day that he was not at school—morning, afternoon, and evening—I had to be on hand to perform his various routines. I was very nearly confined to the house. I could not go away at all except to teach my classes and could not leave overnight. As a long-term consequence, I became what is known as "stuck in mid-career." I was not able to go to conferences, travel to do research, or apply for the tempting academic opportunities that entailed going abroad or, for that matter, going anywhere. The situation might have been ideal, had I been agoraphobic.

Even so, I found myself, in the words of Alexander Pope, "rich ev'n when plunder'd." Good feelings bled into bad—and vice versa. If I were to succinctly sum up the experience of caring for August, it would be with the oxymoron "a woe of ecstasy," a phrase from Emily Dickinson. The words yoke together all the pain, hardship, frustration, love, and joy Ilene and I felt. We were lucky—our son embodied the art of reconciling contradictions. He contained opposites: he was beauty in messiness, shadows and light. In South African English, a sun shower—simultaneous sunshine and rain—is referred to as a "monkey's wedding," a translation of the Zulu phrase *umshado wezinkawu* ("wedding for monkeys"). Our son brought us a wedding for monkeys.

VI

ON A CHILLY NOVEMBER EVENING IN 2005, I positioned myself outside by the doors of the Adam W. Herbert University Center at UNF. A waxing crescent moon dangled on the western horizon. Peter Singer was scheduled to speak in less than one hour. His address was titled "The Changing Ethics of Life and Death." By this point, I considered myself a participant in the disability rights movement. I didn't like protesting, but there I was, quixotically passing out leaflets and holding a protest sign announcing in bold letters "Peter Singer: Deadly for the Disabled." Protesting Singer was something I felt I had to do.

I wasn't challenging Singer's right to speak. But I also had a right to speak—that is, to stand peaceably near the entrance, hold a sign, and pass out leaflets stating my opposition to what he was proposing. I was protesting on behalf of Not Dead Yet, the group I had learned about through Harriet McBryde Johnson's 2003 article in the *New York Times*. Through email I communicated with one of Not Dead Yet's organizers, Stephen Drake. He warned me that sometimes people show up to protest Singer with signs that read "Should Singer Live?"

"We tell them, 'Put those signs away,'" Drake wrote. Tempting as it might have been, we weren't supposed to imply that Singer was not worthy of life. An hour prior to the scheduled time a record crowd was turning out: over nine hundred people would attend that night. Students and fellow faculty were approaching the doors and taking my leaflets. It was a big deal for our university's Department of Philosophy to have brought Singer to campus, so these colleagues weren't thrilled about my little protest.

Like my colleagues, I had always prized intelligence. I was not a candidate for Mensa, but what encouraged me to revere intellect was growing up in Palo Alto, with Stanford less than half a mile from our home and a number of Nobel Prize winners and famous technology innovators living in our neighborhood. People around me had good brains, and that meant money, respect, and international influence. And now I was working in an academic environment that privileged being smart. We academics advanced in our careers by demonstrating how clever we could be, and much depended on flaunting intelligence.

August coming into my life had forced me to question these basic assumptions. We equate intelligence with being human, but he posed for me and all who met or knew of him the provocative question of what it means to be human. For many, someone with his caliber of cognitive and physical impairment created uncertainty about where humanity leaves off and animality begins. This question of where to draw the line had been a major preoccupation of eighteenth-century Enlightenment thinkers. In the twenty-first century, many university scholars and intellectuals would not have considered my son to be human based on his extremely low IQ. But because August was my child, I felt that I had an insight that they didn't have. I realized that framing the question in terms of an animal-human divide was spurious.

This false dichotomy was a product of Enlightenment thinking, and I found myself undertaking an abrupt about-face. I suddenly wanted to reject the entirety of the Enlightenment. *Throw it all out*, I thought angrily, everything that had anything to do with the Enlightenment, but especially its monstrous dreams of reason. Yet I could not sustain this animosity because I immediately had to confront the conundrums of the Enlightenment, for its embedded contradictions make them difficult to resolve. It is not possible to reject the Enlightenment's legacies that we don't like without also rejecting the ones we do. For example, the concept of women's emancipation from patriarchy was rooted in Enlightenment thinking (beginning with Bathsua Makin and Mary Astell and continuing with Sarah Scott and Mary Wollstonecraft), as were the discourses of human rights and individual autonomy.

But therein lay the rub: On the one hand, the inquiries and commitments of Enlightenment rationalism cast doubt on my son's claim to full membership in the human family and so would deny him his rights, even his right to live. On the other, for me to even speak about my son's "human rights" was to draw upon one of the chief legacies of the Enlightenment—the argument that such a thing as human rights exists. Consequently, there is validity in Michel Foucault's assertion (in an article titled "What Is Enlightenment?") that to be for or against the Enlightenment, to either accept or reject its tradition of rationalism, is to engage in a false dichotomy. "We must free ourselves," he writes, "from the intellectual blackmail of 'being for or against the Enlightenment.'"

When Singer started his talk, I left my protest sign outside the door and found what was the last empty seat. Singer projected his PowerPoint on a large screen above his head.

As he was speaking, my overall objection to his approach was still coming into formation. It would be one that philosopher Elizabeth Barnes would express in her book *The Minority Body* a decade later. Singer claims to argue from a position of absolute objective neutrality, but, as Barnes points out, "It's easy to confuse the view from normal with the view from nowhere." I noticed that evening how much he dwelled on the category of personhood. He argued that babies were not yet persons. As noted earlier, for Singer, a person is an entity conscious of itself in relation to time and space and aware that it is mortal. It dawned on me that what Singer was saying was coming straight out of John Locke in his 1689 *Essay Concerning Human Understanding*.

A person, according to Locke, is someone who is conscious of oneself and one's surroundings and location in time, has a long-term memory, and is able to think abstractly. Moreover, a person is able to think and act completely on his own. In no way is he dependent on others. Because such a being had these capabilities, a person possessed a full array of political and legal rights.

When the time came for audience questions and comments, I lined up with many others at the microphone. Each of us was given half a minute. The line was long, and I was near the rear. Already it was late. I had just thirty seconds with Peter Singer. This wasn't much, and I knew that nothing I could say in that short amount of time would throw him back on his heels. My objection to legalizing infanticide was the same as that regarding physician-assisted suicide: all that glitters is not gold. In a nation run by utilitarian conservatives and profit-hungry medical insurance companies, it won't be long before what is being proffered as libertarian "choice" becomes an insidious form of coercion.

Almost everyone ahead of me in the line voiced objections rooted in Christian teaching. Many quoted the scriptures, and their questions amounted to pretty much the same one: "What is your foundation?" In other words, what was his foundation in religious faith? I knew very well that this line of inquiry wasn't going to get anywhere with a committed atheist like Singer. Not that I had any silver bullets. Because I had not been trained as a philosopher, I really didn't know what to say, and I wasn't terribly confident that I wasn't going to make a fool of myself. When I finally got up to the mic, I froze for a second. The only thing I could think of to say was to point out that his notion of *person* stemmed from Locke's *Essay*. That was aiming my arrow pretty low. Locke was the first philosopher to use the word *person* in the way that Singer was now using it.

Singer more or less agreed.

"And isn't it true," I said, suddenly thinking of something else, "that Locke, the philosopher who was the first to define *person* in the way that you are now using the term—didn't he consider nonpersons—his word was *changelings*—didn't he conclude that changeling infants should not be put to death?"

Once more he agreed.

And then I thought of another thing to say: "And didn't he also say that changelings at birth should be allowed to live because no one at the time when they are born knows precisely what the future holds, that some changelings may grow up to become abstract thinkers? That we can't know for certain which of them will think abstractly and which won't? And didn't he ultimately conclude that, in humility, we should defer to what we don't know? That we should err on the side of caution? We should let them live?"

Singer conceded that, yes, this was Locke's position.

And then my time was up. Nobody applauded as I walked back to my seat. Probably the only people in the auditorium who understood our exchange were Singer and a few people in the Philosophy Department. I felt that I had completely let down Not Dead Yet. My objections to Singer's position were too technical to be widely understood.

What should I have said? I should have confronted him about his ableist bias. I should have drawn attention to the fact that he was reinforcing the dichotomies of abnormal and normal and disabled and nondisabled, and that he was paying uncritical deference to norms of human function. I should have spoken out that it is not just people with "normal" bodies and "orderly" thought processes who have a right to live (how many of us would survive *that* test!). I should have argued that his support for euthanizing babies is based not in reason but on prejudice. I should have insisted that disability was not some infrequently encountered exception but an integral aspect of the human condition. I should have pointed out that the majority of disabilities are acquired, not congenital. I should have stressed that being human is not a matter of either/or but of both/and, a spectrum of variation.

But, most importantly, I should have said, "How dare you suggest that my son is less than fully human."

When I was a young university student, Hamlet's famous statement to his friend puzzled me: "There are more things in heaven and earth, Horatio, Than are dreamt of in your philosophy." Back then I had believed that philosophy was the highest order of human thinking. How could it leave anything out? That night in November 2005, though, I realized that philosophers like Singer could not dream of August in their philosophies. If more of them were going to include him in their dreams, they first would have to imagine him in their waking hours.

Philosopher Martha Nussbaum's book *Frontiers of Justice* would not come out until the following year. In it she would articulate the position that I myself was coming to, based on my interactions with August. Speaking with regard to the daughter of fellow philosopher Eva Feder Kittay, Sesha, whose condition is not dissimilar to August's, Nussbaum writes, "The fact that she has a human body and is the child of two human parents plays a large role here." But more importantly, she states,

> To the extent that we do think of Sesha's life as a human life, and I think we are not deceived when we do, it is presumably because at least some of the most important human capabilities are manifest in it, and these capabilities link her to the human community rather than some other: the ability to love and relate to others, perception, delight in movement and play.

Nussbaum seems more inclined to view humanity as a spectrum of variation, and so, by her standard, August and Sesha occupy a place on it. Singer does not accept this view. For him, full humanity is a matter of a binary opposition: an entity is either fully human or it is not at all. The linearity of his thinking amazed and continues to amaze me. There are no shades of gray, no gradations between one extreme and its opposite, no variability. For him, it is a matter of black or white.

It was a hot Saturday morning in late July 2005. Clio was three and a half years old, and August was six. He was wearing an orange Reese's Pieces T-shirt and beige shorts. Two hundred or more people had assembled in tree-shaded Hemming Park across from Jacksonville's city hall. These were disabled people, activists, and supporters of the disability rights movement who actively fought against disablism. One of its slogans was "Nothing about us without us"; these words meant that disabled people want to have a major voice in the decisions that are made in their name and that impact their lives. Today would be our pride march, Crip Pride.

Clio, Ilene, and I were there as supporters, as temporarily able-bodied people, and August was present as one of the disabled. We all had come together to celebrate the fourteenth anniversary of President George H. W. Bush's signing of the Americans with Disabilities Act (ADA).

Before the march began, our family was going to meet August's new friend, Ronnie, a young man living with cerebral palsy. This was an important moment because August hadn't had any friends. Ronnie was considerably older, and he reminded me of Larry Buchalter from Dr. Voloshin's class at San Francisco State. Buchalter returned fully to my memory, as did my curt dismissal of him on the phone. But this madeleine dipped in tea did not taste sweet, for I now saw Larry in a different light. There was no escaping the conclusion that I had been a bigot. Back in 1989, I could not imagine what life was like from his point of view. His critical comments about John Locke indicated that he had a penetrating mind, and a conversation at the student union about this philosopher would have been edifying. At the time I didn't consider how much effort Larry had to put into activities that are easy for most people. And I didn't ask myself what opportunities would be available for him once he earned his degree. It didn't occur to me that people with serious impairments who are successful in college often don't find work once they graduate.

These concerns and insights now transferred to Ronnie. He had gone to school his whole life at Mt. Herman, but the preceding year, at twenty-two, he had aged out. He shouldn't have been enrolled there at all because every other child in the school lived with severe cognitive impairment, and Ronnie was reputed to be brilliant. Duval County Public Schools (the local school district) probably had placed him there because he was a spastic quadriplegic. Provision should have been made for him: a one-on-one aide should have been assigned, and he should have attended one of the district's magnet schools for gifted children.

After Ronnie had aged out, the Mt. Herman staff found a job for him at the school, part of which entailed working with August. Our son had become one of his favorites, and I was eager to meet this young man who liked him so much.

In Hemming Park, we quickly picked him and his mother out of the crowd. Unkempt dark hair against pale skin, Ronnie was small and slender, his body slightly curved in his power chair. His limbs were thin, his chin and upper lip were heavily whiskered, and his expression was gentle. Although he could hardly move, I could tell from his lively glance that he was busy taking everything in. The following year, after spending six weeks in the hospital, Ronnie would die of pneumonia. But that was still in the future. Ronnie on that day of the ADA march was still very much with us, and it was a fine day to be alive. I took a good look at him. He had an Adam's apple, a man's jaw, and broad shoulders. These were foreshadowings, for up until this moment I hadn't thought at all about what August might be like once he became a man. It shocked me that in a few years I would have to start shaving him.

When the march got underway we advanced southward on Laura Street. It was hot, and we needed hats now to provide some shade. While I pushed August in his Zippie manual wheelchair, Ronnie motored alongside. August laughed at the things he said.

Clio was excited by what she called "the parade," for that's what it was for her. By turns she held her mother's hand, helped me push August, rode on August's lap, and hopped, pranced, and skipped along. Ahead of and around us was a sea of humanity. There were the rolling quads. There were wheelchair folks. There were people striding confidently with white canes and propelling themselves jerkily on account of cerebral palsy and walking with service animals beside them.

After the march, when we returned home, Clio constructed pipe-cleaner wheelchairs for her dolls. She also made her wooden dollhouse ADA-compliant by retrofitting it with ramps. The dolls were able to wheel freely in and out of the little rooms. Crip Pride had been brought home to the dollhouse.

VII

DURING THE MIDDLE AGES, THE WORD *MONSTER* referred to something that was unintelligible. (Here I am drawing on David Williams's book, *Deformed Discourse*.) The monstrous was not so much something frightening like Godzilla or the Thing in the Crate as something incomprehensible and awe-inspiring, a wonder or prodigy. As such, it served to signify the inscrutable nature of God. It was a sign of his mysterious ways. However, just before and during the Enlightenment, *monster* began to stand for something else, for a radical, terrible, and frightening deviation from the typical or expected.

For many people who encountered August but didn't get to know him well, he was a monster in the latter sense. He was a being so exaggeratedly different that he made them feel uncomfortable. There were parents in Jacksonville who didn't want their children to come over to our house to play with Clio because a boy in a wheelchair lived inside. It wasn't just a Jacksonville problem, of course. Some of the affluent parents whose children attended the Child Care Center at Presidio Heights—such as Rachel's mother—had not wanted their children to associate with August. Still a child, he had been stigmatized. To them he was Boo Radley, someone to protect their children from.

For those who did come to know August well, he was a monster in the former sense: he was inscrutable. This inability to fathom him, to solve his mystery, eventually would bring to mind questions not so much about him but about the nature of meaning itself. Looking into his eyes represented gazing directly at the mystery of the universe—at least this was true for me and for a few others. To the extent that he would provoke large questions, he became a child signifying the unfathomable cosmos. This is not to say that his disability conveyed a meaning but rather that it disrupted meaning. He exposed the limits of meaning, the illusory nature of the meaning-making enterprise. His disability compelled me to stand in awe of everything, of a universe stripped of the significance that we human beings impose on it.

What would happen if I were to resort to John Keats's "negative capability," leaving off irritable reaching after fact and reason and instead pondering the totality of everything— the earth and moon and stars and, beyond these, the infinite and the eternal, without a ready set of answers? Would this be to enter into a truly spiritual state?

Over time I gained the beginnings of an answer. Several times while changing August's diaper, I became entranced. I had the weird sensation while looking into my son's hazel eyes that I was staring into the face of God. Each time this would feel like it was going on for as much as half a minute, but it probably lasted no longer than a green flash at sunset. As a nonbeliever, I didn't know what to think. And I still don't. Someone with my education and philosophical orientation and profession should have no truck with mystical flights of fancy. Was I losing my mind?

August's daily routine was sometimes tedious and always time-consuming. Attending to a hyper-maintenance child could be a grind, and transporting a quadriplegic, even a miniature one, could be difficult. You might think that fathering such a child would supply an atheist dad with all the more proof that there is no God. These face-of-God moments may have been the strangest surprise of the entire adventure. Despite the monotony and incessant worry, these rare moments while looking into his eyes provided the most intense apprehensions of life I had ever experienced.

Let me put it another way: at times my son would be lying supine on his extra-large changing table, and I would suddenly be "hanging ten," as the surfers say, tube riding within the barrel of a breaking wave. Like the ones at Banzai Pipeline, the water would form a moving cylinder as it broke, its curl overhanging me. I would be hurling lengthwise beneath it, headlong through the tube, surrounded by a violent swelling upheaval of windmill-wings blue. At the end of the tunnel toward which I was speeding would be a small bright circle of Laughing Orange.

These colorful reveries were exhilarating, but my skepticism would kick in after the wave collapsed. Probably all this psychedelic potency was just intense fatigue exploding within me, wires in the brain crossing, the material consequence of being chronically sleep-deprived and stressed.

But what if it was something more? If God exists, was this one of his little jokes? Was he giving me a vision while changing a poopy diaper? I had heard Christians say that God uses the difficult, awkward, and silly circumstances of our lives to teach us about grace and redemption. Was this what was happening?

Whichever it was, the cosmos or craziness, I found myself to be an atheist who was already well along the path of a spiritual journey. There was no turning back now. But even if whatever it was I experienced turned out to be something more, something transcendental, I didn't intend to start proselytizing. I was not going to found a religious sect based on it. If I did, distributing the communion sacrament for my new church would have been particularly noisome.

Lucy Grealy writes, "The general plot of life is sometimes shaped by the different ways genuine intelligence combines with equally genuine ignorance." Her words about intelligence and ignorance combining to shape events apply here. Although I grew up in Silicon Valley and imbibed its ideology like mother's milk, I have become skeptical regarding high technology on account of what happened, which I will speak about now. What I took to be the *cutting edge* turned out to be the *bleeding edge*.

In 2003 Dr. Achilles Joyce was recruited to run the first pediatric neurosurgery program in northeast Florida. A multimillion-dollar endowment made founding it possible. The internationally recognized Dr. Joyce, originally from Argentina, had been practicing medicine for four decades, much of that time at a teaching hospital associated with the University of California. Having recently retired, Joyce had accepted an offer from the medical school of a nearby university to come open a clinic at Bensalem-Salomon Children's Hospital (a pseudonym).

Achilles Joyce headed to northeast Florida to begin building a program, recruiting other pediatric neurosurgeons from around the nation. His name and reputation were the attraction. And this is how the area's first Relaxanoid implantable infusion pump program came into existence. Manufactured by Hippocrates, the Relaxanoid pump was a piece of science fiction wizardry come true.

One of the physicians Dr. Joyce recruited was a physiatrist specializing in spasticity management. Spasticity, by the way, is the major component of cerebral palsy. At Dr. Joyce's behest, Dr. Lisa Sandemelir moved from the Midwest to northeast Florida with her husband and two small children. Simultaneously vivacious and relaxed, Sandemelir smiled easily, and her demeanor set us at ease. Only years later did I realize that she was the lure.

Ilene and I first met with her in January 2008 at a clinic in a tall building adjacent to Bensalem-Salomon. August was nine years old at the time. To get him onto the examining table, I first I had to scoop him out of his wheelchair. She had me lay August face up on a cushioned examining table with a white towel under his head and body. "As he grows older," she informed us as she measured the range of motion in his left leg, "his problems are going to become more complicated and harder to manage."

She laid the left leg down and moved to the right one, flexing it at the knee, and said, "Increasing spasticity will bring on more muscle tightening." August cooed with pleasure as she manipulated him. Watching her work with our son, I could see that she was gentle and kind. These qualities impressed me. They made me trust her.

August was beginning to experience painful charley horses when sitting in his wheelchair. He would suddenly cry out and push up from the foot pedals with both legs. Over the years, since the age of five, he had undergone several surgeries, one of them an adductor release. He had briefly been considered for a rhizotomy (a neurosurgical procedure that selectively destroys problematic nerve roots coming off the spinal cord) to relieve the symptoms of spastic cerebral palsy. This procedure was ruled out because his physicians concluded that he was not a good candidate. They didn't explain why.

As a course of treatment, Dr. Sandemelir prescribed powdered Relaxanoid to be taken orally with his meals, and this helped with the leg cramping. She also started him on a regimen of periodic off-label Botox injections into his upper legs, hips, thighs, and lower back. The two worked extremely well in relieving August's spasticity. For six to eight weeks the shots would alleviate the muscle spasms, but then the effects of Botox would begin to wear off. I then would have to take August back to Sandemelir's clinic for a new set of Botox injections. These visits occurred once every three months. Taking the injections didn't bother August. He didn't cry about receiving them because, unlike typically developing children, he didn't know that the needle was coming. For him the process was over as soon as it began. With each injection, he might briefly wince or purse his lips, but he never cried.

During a clinic visit in November 2009, Dr. Sandemelir changed the tenor of her medical advice. Four of us were present at this visit: the doctor, August, me, and a short, stocky, red-faced, middle-aged man—a Hippocrates company rep. He introduced himself and shook my hand with a grip that was firm and steady. I would see him a few times in the years that followed. Because I could never remember his long name, I thought of him as the Yellow Man because he always wore a pale yellow dress shirt.

Dr. Sandemelir told me that afternoon that she had two effective methods in her tool kit for treating children with spasticity. They were the periodic off-label Botox injections with Relaxanoid daily by mouth, the regimen we were pursuing, and alternatively an implanted pump. The pump was an astonishingly high-tech innovation. The combination of Botox injections with oral Relaxanoid was the opposite: it was effective but low-tech. In the years since, I have come to appreciate that the term *low-tech* carries pejorative connotations. The online Urban Dictionary lists these hashtags for its slang use: #stupid, #slow, #idiotic, #dumb, and #dim, all of which point to one of modernity's fundamental prejudices.

During our conversation, and with the company rep present, Dr. Sandemelir began nudging me to abandon the injections in favor of implanting a pump. Nothing in August's medical profile had changed requiring the transition, but the ease of the pump was what she emphasized. I wouldn't have to bring August into her clinic every three months for the next set of shots.

In her presentation she was upbeat, her voice inflected with optimism. The issue, she explained, was that when Relaxanoid is taken orally, most of the drug stays in the bloodstream. The targeted area for the drug was the cerebrospinal fluid (CSF) that bathes the spinal cord and the brain. When taken by mouth, only a small amount of it reaches the CSF, even at very high doses. Additionally, high doses of Relaxanoid are toxic to the body's other organs, such as the kidneys and liver.

Speaking in a pleasant tone and projecting a "can do" attitude, she said, "The pump bypasses these organs by injecting liquid Relaxanoid directly into the cerebrospinal fluid." As she went on explaining the benefits of the device, I could tell that she really wanted Ilene and me to give up relying on Botox injections to manage August's spasticity. She was pushing the pump.

Dr. Sandemelir continued with what was turning into a sales pitch. She brought out a laminated card the size of a sheet of paper. Explaining the two diagrams on it, she walked me step by step through them. It was a color illustration of what the pump arrangement would look like anatomically, two angles of the same human subject, one facing forward, the other in profile. Visible in both the front and side views was a circular reservoir smaller than a hockey puck implanted under the skin of the two figures' lower abdomen. A catheter then ran internally (within the body) from the reservoir in the front of the body around to the back, to the lumbar area (above the buttocks), entered the canal surrounding the spinal column and threaded within the canal up to about the midpoint of the thoracic spine (below the shoulders). There, within the spinal column canal, in an area called the intrathecal space, liquid Relaxanoid would emerge from the catheter tip in a slow drip and mix with the CSF surrounding the spinal cord. The CSF, with the drug Relaxanoid diffused into it, eventually would spread up into the CSF surrounding the brain, the target for the drug.

Laying the card aside, she said, "When Relaxanoid is supplied this way, the patient needs less of it, and this minimizes some of the drug's negative side effects such as drowsiness, nausea, low blood pressure, and dizziness, not to leave out the drug's toxic effect on the other organs."

She paused for a moment to let this information sink in, then resumed. "There is also the matter of convenience. You will only have to come in once every six months. The Relaxanoid pump reservoir only needs to be replenished with liquid Relaxanoid roughly twice a year."

She informed me that she or her physician assistant, Ms. Bosman, would refill it. One or the other of them would insert a needle through the skin to the reservoir (located to the side of August's lower abdomen) just below the skin's surface and inject a fresh supply of Relaxanoid into it using a syringe. Setting the dosage of liquid Relaxanoid entering the patient's spinal fluid would be regulated wirelessly via remote control. At this point, she showed me the remote control, and she let me hold it, but for no more than ten seconds, as though it were precious.

She described for me the long-term benefits, in essence what would be the payoff. "With reduced systemic spasticity," she said, "August might be able to gain sufficient motor control to feed himself. With occupational therapy he may eventually be able to guide a spoon into a bowl and bring the food to his mouth. He won't need to be hand-fed. Not at first, of course," she cautioned, "but with occupational therapy. Immediately following the surgery he would spend two weeks as an inpatient at the Brooks Rehabilitation Center here in Jacksonville."

"With therapy," she continued, "he should be able to walk more naturally in his gait trainer, as opposed to what he is doing now." Currently he was thrusting himself forward with spasmodic, jerky motions.

"I don't know," I said. "The pump's probably too expensive for us."

"The Relaxanoid pump is not experimental. Your insurance plan will approve the pump, its implantation, the two weeks of therapy at Brooks, and all of the follow-up. With your PPO plan, it will cover 80 percent of these expenses, and Medicaid will pick up the remaining 20 percent."

"Is the pump dangerous?" I said. "It seems terribly complicated."

"These pumps represent a sophisticated approach to managing spasticity," she told me. "They have been in common use for well over a decade. Dozens of children living in the local area now have them." In essence, she was telling me that the pump was reasonably safe, almost as safe as riding in an airplane. Having a pump implanted in our son was just about worry free.

"But are they really safe?" I persisted.

At this point the Yellow Man looked me straight in the eye and assured me that the pump was a safe product. If Ilene and I decided to go with it, he went on, he personally would accompany us "on each step of the journey." Everything would go well—he would "make certain." He would "see to it."

When I spoke with Ilene that night about the pump, she was full of doubt. In fact, she flat out didn't like the idea. She had been made cynical about medicine after having given birth to August in one of the world's finest hospitals.

Ilene wasn't able to attend these appointments with Dr. Sandemelir. My employment at the university allowed me more flexibility than her job did. I could work late at night or early in the morning, whereas her patients had to see her during regular business hours. Working in a physical therapy practice she didn't own meant that she was paid hourly. For each hour she took off from work, she had to cancel an appointment with a patient, and doing so meant not getting paid for that hour. Given our shaky finances due to the high cost of August's care, canceling patients was not an option.

At the next appointment, when it was just Dr. Sandemelir, August, and I, the doctor didn't want to dwell on the pump's potential hazards. When I pressed her a little more, she conceded that there had been some problems when the pumps first came on the market over a decade earlier. But she immediately reassured me, saying, "We've come a long way since then." The only perils she would admit to were minimal and manageable, having mainly to do with the pump hardware having been known to malfunction or the catheter kinking. But about these problems she remained vague. How many pumps overall had the pediatric neurosurgery program implanted? She couldn't produce a number. Could Ilene and I speak with other parents whose children had received the pump? No, we couldn't: HIPAA (the Health Insurance and Portability and Accountability Act of 1996) prohibited giving out names, she said. How many pumps had the program been forced to remove, for whatever reason? She couldn't say.

That night I said to Ilene, "This is what the doctor tells me August needs." She still didn't like the pump, but gradually she began to reconsider the matter. She and I deliberated for months. In fact, we agonized. What inclined me to favor the pump? The mysterious, handsome, and charismatic Dr. Joyce had an impressive publishing record; he was highly accomplished, the expert's expert. And Dr. Sandemelir's medical training was fresh, and her pitch was seductive. Through a kind of rhetorical hocus-pocus, she was able to alchemically transform a mere mechanical implement into a medical marvel. It was as though she were pulling back the curtain and allowing me to glimpse a scene from the future.

Overall, what Dr. Sandemelir and Dr. Joyce offered was terribly appealing. I trusted them because they were operating this university program through Bensalem-Salomon—a *children's* hospital and a beloved local institution. No one in the community doubted for a second that it was doing good and important work. To even suspect that the motives of its physicians or the institution itself might not be 100 percent honorable and altruistic would have been blasphemy.

I asked around about the pump. At Mt. Herman (August's school) and the DLC Nurse & Learn, where he went after school, I mentioned it to one person after another, other parents and the teachers and staff. From them I detected muffled, generalized complaints. However, no specific game-changing horror story ever came to light. It was as if people didn't like the pump, but they couldn't say why. Nor could I find anything damning about the Relaxanoid pump on the Internet. I Googled repeatedly, using one set of search-term combinations after another, but nothing negative turned up. Had Jeanne Lenzer's book *The Danger Within Us: America's Untested, Unregulated Medical Device Industry* been published, or the Netflix documentary about medical devices, *The Bleeding Edge*, been released, I would have been warned. But Lenzer's book would not come out until 2017, and the documentary not until 2018—seven and eight years, respectively, in the future. Consequently, the premonitions of ill fortune were like household moths—it was hard to locate where they were breeding.

On the other side of the question were Dr. Sandemelir and the positive persuasion she brought to bear. She was a techno optimist, and her enthusiasm was infectious. And then there was the pump itself. The very device inspired awe, and the fantasy gripped me. It made possible a beautiful vision, one in which August would be transfigured. His flesh and bone would become entwined with a digital-mechanical device. Our boy would become a citizen of the brave new world, a hybrid of sentient being and machine, a technological human. My latent transhumanism—my own dormant ableism—came to the surface in vivid, futuristic fantasies. I envisioned August breaking free of his chrysalis to embody a new genre of human being—the cyborg.

Ilene rearranged her patient schedule and managed to attend one of August's doctor's appointments. And so, late one afternoon in May 2010, the four of us—Dr. Stephen Cohen—August's regular pediatrician, August himself, and his parents—occupied one of the small examining rooms in the pediatric group practice to which Dr. Cohen belonged, located just off San Jose Boulevard near Baymeadows in the Mandarin neighborhood. Dr. Cohen was an older physician nearing retirement. I knew that he cared deeply about August. Back in 2001, when our family moved from San Francisco to Jacksonville, he had agreed to take August on as a patient in part because of our mutual Stanford connection. He had served his residency in the Stanford Medical Center, and I had earned my PhD in Stanford's English department. But he also wanted August as his patient because he wished to accept the challenge that a boy like him would pose.

Ilene opened the appointment by explaining the reason why we had come. Dr. Cohen then repeated her words slowly and carefully, as if unsure that he had heard her correctly. "The Hippocrates Relaxanoid pump," he said. The stress lines of his face seemed to deepen. It was as though the very words troubled him. After a long pause, he said again, "The Hippocrates Relaxanoid pump," but this time with certainty and with thinly veiled contempt. He looked down at the floor, from the floor to the ceiling, ceiling to floor. Finally, he looked up, first at Ilene, then at me, and said, "Be very careful."

Ilene and I stood there, waiting for more. Finally, she said, "For me, as a physical therapist and a mom, the biggest selling point is that the spasticity is masking his function. And if he had the Relaxanoid pump and went to rehab at Brooks to maximize his function, he would have a chance to do more. We as his parents should let him have this chance to do all he can, to move and to communicate with us."

Dr. Cohen nodded as he listened to her.

"And the Relaxanoid pump," she continued, "would help with all that pushing up into standing he does while in his wheelchair. He breaks straps and the foot pedals of his wheelchair doing this. He even once broke off his headrest. He would stay more comfortable in his wheelchair, when he is riding on the school bus and sitting at school and for feedings."

Dr. Cohen was taking all of this in.

"The Relaxanoid pump," she went on, "would decrease the scissoring of his legs when we are doing diaper changes and when he is trying to walk in his Rifton. It would save him from the 'charley horse effect,' which is just the spasticity tightening up his leg muscles."

Dr. Cohen asked, "Has the charley horse effect continued with the Botox injections?"

"Botox is managing it," she said. "But Chris is August's primary caregiver, and his having to go into Dr. Sandemelir's office so often for the Botox injections inconveniences him. Because of the herniated disc in my neck, he has to do all of the therapy and doctors' appointments. He goes almost every week to one appointment or another for August. And that's on top of doing a lot of August's morning and bedtime routine, his feeding, hygiene, dressing, and bathing. And that's not to mention taking him to school every morning and picking him up almost every afternoon. That's a lot of time out of his work week."

What followed then was Dr. Cohen's sober appraisal. "Nothing is inherently wrong with the device itself, at least that I'm aware of at this time," he said. "The problem is with the highly invasive procedure that implanting it requires."

I broke in, "But if it can relieve his spasticity..." I thought Dr. Cohen was being too cautious, too conservative, *too old*. I added, "What could go wrong?"

"A lot can go wrong," he said in a short tone betraying impatience with my naïveté. He went on to say that patients of his who had entered the Bensalem-Salomon pump program had experienced difficulties. "Major problems," he said. "Whenever you go into the back like that, you run the risk of serious unintended consequences."

"But they *do* work," I insisted.

"The pump is an aggressive approach," he said firmly. "It's a highly invasive procedure. There's a simpler one available that's close to equally effective, and that's the treatment Augie's currently on—Botox. You do know, don't you, that you can go on indefinitely using Botox and achieve the same therapeutic effect as the pump? There have been some adverse effects with Botox, but, if I had to choose between the pump and Botox, I'd choose Botox. The risk is negligible compared to the pump."

"Are you against it because it's high tech?" I asked.

"No," he shot back, "but I don't cut my steak with a chainsaw either."

"But the pump would be so much easier. I wouldn't have to go into Dr. Sandemelir's office every three months. I'd only have to go in every six months."

"The pump is the impressive 'go-big-or-go-home' option," he countered. "We Americans don't think well of ourselves if we don't 'go big or go home.' We want to go full throttle all of the time. We want the most aggressive solution there is. Anything less, we think, is half-hearted—we worry that we're not doing all that we can. But in medicine, believe me, sometimes less is better."

We all stood there silently for a moment, except of course for August. He was cooing as he sat strapped into his wheelchair and played with a toy secured with a bungee cord to the tray in front of him. Finally, Ilene said, "What are the things that can go wrong?"

"Infection is the main problem," the doctor replied. "And problems with the back, the spinal column. A lot can go wrong when you go into the back. But any number of things. I wish I could tell you more. HIPAA restrictions, you see, prohibit me from discussing specific cases with you. But, believe me, a lot can go wrong."

I didn't say anything, but I remember thinking, *If there's an infection, they'll treat it with antibiotics and make it go away.*

Dr. Cohen then added that August was a particularly bad candidate for a pump—his nonverbal status, he believed, should disqualify him. Two days earlier, Dr. Sandemelir had addressed this very concern. She had underscored that August's disabilities—his nonverbal status—should not keep him out of the pump program. Dr. Sandemelir had said, "August has as much right to a pump as any typically developing child."

But this day Dr. Cohen pointed out that August, being nonverbal, wouldn't be able to tell anyone how the pump was making him feel. And how and what he felt would be an important factor in helping Dr. Sandemelir find the right dosage of Relaxanoid. "The speed of the pump is how the dose is determined," he informed us.

"Yes. It's wireless," I said. "They use a remote control. I know because she let me hold it."

At this he gave me a look as though I were an imbecile. And then he said, "Without a verbal cue from the patient, how's Dr. Sandemelir going to know at what speed to set it? Doing this right requires constantly adjusting the speed in light of the patient's spoken response."

"Clinical observation," I said.

"But if Augie can't tell her what or how he feels, I don't see how she's going to be able to do that."

"Clinical observation," I repeated.

"Will that be enough?"

"I've been told it will be."

"But I don't think it will be. He'll be a black box. By your own admission, Dr. Sandemelir is only going to see him once every six months. How can she possibly do any clinical observation if she hardly ever sees him? And you as the parents, how are you going to be able to judge? It will be up to you to perform the 'clinical observation.'"

He paused for a moment, then said, "No! I don't like the sound of this at all! Putting a pump in Augie will be like launching an astronaut into space without giving him a way to communicate. Bad things could happen, but he'd never have a way to tell anyone."

Ilene entered the conversation at this point, saying, "So you don't think the pump is a good idea." She was repeating

Dr. Cohen's sentiment for the sake of clarity, to help herself absorb it.

Turning to her, he said, "I have seen so much go wrong." I remember thinking, *If so much has gone wrong, why isn't that information available on the Internet?* I didn't realize that, in three more years, the stories of trouble would begin to appear there.

Then he faced me and looked at me straight in the eye and sternly held my gaze the way a wise father does when trying to get through to his thickheaded son. He was doing this for my own good and for August's. If grabbing and shaking me had stood a chance of changing my mind, he would have done it. If slapping me would have gotten the point across, he might have done that too.

But instead he tried using psychology. "You're an English professor, am I correct? And a Stanford man. Then you should know your Shakespeare. Do you remember what Albany said in *King Lear*? Albany says to Goneril, 'Striving to better, oft we mar what's well.'"

He wanted this advice to sink in. We stood a moment longer, our gazes locked. "I'd keep this maxim in mind," he finally said.

Dr. Cohen continued looking me in the eye several seconds longer, then nodded and turned away when he realized that he had made no impression on me whatsoever.

What is the nature of informed consent? It is supposed to mean that patients or their parents and guardians (or both) are made aware of all of the dangers beforehand so that they can make a reasoned, educated choice. What did informed consent look like in this real-life situation involving our own child? In his book *Doctored: The Disillusionment of an American Physician*, Sandeep Jauhar points out that "studies have shown that patients take little interest in the informed consent process." This may be true, but physicians also can be glib.

Ilene finally came around and agreed to having the pump implanted. She had lived a long time in the Bay Area, as I had, and there is something about living in that part of the world that makes people a little too eager to embrace high technology. I suspect it's the razzle-dazzle that comes with thinking that we are living on the edge of the future. She was as susceptible to this as I was.

A week before the procedure to implant the pump, our friend Dr. Arnold Graham-Smith, at the time a practicing surgeon, advised us to request seventy-two hours of antibiotics during the immediate post-surgery period. He informed us that this longer amount of time would help prevent infection. But when we asked Dr. Joyce about it, he responded by saying that Bensalem-Salomon had a strict protocol requiring him not to exceed twenty-four. Later, when we told Arnold about this time limit, he simply winced.

At 9 a.m. on July 8, 2010, Dr. Joyce began the surgery that implanted the Relaxanoid pump. On the day of the surgery I did not speak with the Yellow Man, but he was present in the operating room while the pump was being implanted. Company reps for Hippocrates and other medical device makers, I was learning, frequently did this. People in this line of work, often without having much or any medical training, earn substantial six-figure salaries. After the surgery and then time in the recovery room, August was wheeled in a hospital bed back into the room where I was waiting for him. We had been assigned to a room in

Bensalem-Salomon's west wing on a floor known as Five West. He was still heavily sedated.

After several days of closely monitored convalescence at Bensalem-Salomon, August was supposed to go, as a follow-up, for two weeks of intensive therapy as an inpatient at Brooks Rehab. Ilene and I had been led to believe that during these two weeks physical and occupational therapists would help August learn how to feed himself, as Dr. Sandemelir had suggested. August, though, while still at the hospital, was experiencing so much pain that he could not undergo therapy. He cried and cried and cried.

While August was still an inpatient at Bensalem-Salomon, the decision was made that he could not go to Brooks because his discomfort level was too great. So we took him home. When I wheeled him in during the first month of weekly post-op visits with Dr. Sandemelir, he often would be wailing at the top of his lungs. Struggling with the presence of a large foreign object in his body, he was crying in a way that I had not seen or heard since his first two and a half years of life.

After a month or so, August calmed sufficiently to the point that he was able to go to school at Mt. Herman. The school year started during the third week of August, and, as he had always done during his many years prior, he went to the DLC Nurse & Learn after the school day was over. He usually spent from an hour and a half to two hours there at the end of each day, and I would pick him up between 5:30 and 6 p.m. to take him home. His providers, Eric Conger and Nancy Frias, took great care of him. They were dependable and conscientious, and I could relax during this time, knowing that he was in good hands.

The difficulty began seven weeks after the surgery, at the end of the month, on August 27, a Friday. When I came through the DLC door at about 5:45 p.m., Nancy and Eric approached with worried looks. When Eric had been changing August's diaper just minutes earlier, he'd noticed something troubling. The surgical incision site at the base of August's spine had opened ever so slightly, just a pinhole of a break in the skin, and what alarmed Eric was the fact that pus was slowly oozing out.

This discharge was starting over a month post-op, and that really worried me. Immediately I drove August to Bensalem-Salomon, where he was readmitted. But my speed in getting him back into the hospital didn't matter, since he and I then spent the entire weekend waiting in a room on Five West for someone from the pediatric neurosurgery program to come through the hospital room door and address the problem. Finally, on Monday morning, Dr. Joyce strode in with an air of busy importance and did a brief inspection. The pus that was oozing out was, he said, actually cerebrospinal fluid (CSF), the liquid that was supposed to remain within his spinal cord canal and brain cavity. He also announced that the pump site had become infected, and this meant that the oozing fluid was not just CSF but also runoff from the infection. He then informed me that this was not an insurmountable or even a serious problem. The next day, to cleanse the pump, he performed major surgery requiring general anesthesia, opening August up to "disinfect" the hardware. Afterward he began flooding August's system with antibiotics.

Dr. Joyce's first operation to disinfect the pump didn't work. The site remained infected, and the CSF continued oozing out. In the next weeks—and months—three more major surgeries would be devoted just to trying to stop the leak and cleaning the pump. I was learning on the fly just how frequently implanted hardware of one kind or another leads to infection. This would have been helpful to know before consenting to implantation of the pump. Dr. Cohen had said something about infection, but I hadn't grasped just how extensive, serious, and difficult to treat such problems were. Artificial knees, hips, shoulders, deep-brain stimulators, anything human-made that is put into the body is subject to infection. And once it turns septic, it is hard to disinfect because the synthetic material doesn't respond to antibiotics in the same way that natural tissue does.

Slowly the realization dawned: I had done my research, but I hadn't asked the right question. Months earlier I had gone online looking for information about Relaxanoid pumps but hadn't found anything negative. I thought that I was performing due diligence. But in addition to seeking information about pumps, I should also have been investigating the success rates of implanted hardware. Hardware infection in general was the issue, not the specific pump.

Each operation to clean the pump was supposed to be the last one. August would go in for a cleansing surgery, remain in the hospital as an inpatient during a recovery period, and then return home. Ilene and I would hope that the infection would abate. When it didn't, we would head back to the hospital for another operation.

So frequently was August a hospital resident that he had to have a peripherally inserted central catheter (or PICC line) put in. This was a long-term semipermanent central IV line entering his body on the right side of his neck. Having it there eliminated the need to stick IV lines into his arms or hands, where they would become detached with maddening frequency. It sometimes would take a nurse up to fifteen minutes to get a new "stick." Between surgeries, when he was at home with the PICC line, our house became a mini hospital, with the appropriate syringes, gauzes, and sterilization equipment laid out on a special tray. Four times a day, six hours apart, we had to inject antibiotic into his PICC line.

This procedure had to be undertaken with extreme care. Not only did all the items have to be immaculately clean, but with each injection we had to avoid letting an air bubble creep into the fluid. A bubble could go directly to his heart and kill him. At least this was the extreme danger impressed upon us. Administering the 2 a.m. antibiotic was a nerve-racking experience. Knowing that a mistake could kill our child demanded focus. Going back to sleep afterward proved difficult.

I had first gotten to know the insides of Bensalem-Salomon back in December 2001, within months of our having moved to Jacksonville from San Francisco. Clio had just been born when August came down with a mysterious ailment that the physicians had trouble diagnosing. Bensalem-Salomon assigned August to the fifth floor of a relatively newer section of the hospital known as "The Tower." Referencing the infamous Tower of London, I quipped to Ilene that August was an innocent man who had been sent to the Tower. Ilene was told not to visit because she was nursing Clio, and the doctors feared that whatever August had might be transmitted to her and then the baby. So I spent the entire time with August and rarely went home. After two weeks of mulling it over, his doctors decided that he must have been suffering from Stevens-Johnson syndrome. This is a severe skin disorder stemming from an allergic reaction to an antibiotic, but in August's case it also involved an autoimmune disorder. August was given a steroid shot, he almost instantly returned to normal (or "normal" at least for August), and the syndrome never came back. He and I wound up going home on Christmas Eve. Christmas Day that year was my sweetest ever.

Over the ensuing decade, but before the Relaxanoid pump implantation, August would spend several nights in the hospital, but what I'd discovered in 2001 held true for the summer and fall of 2010. Once again, Bensalem-Salomon assigned August to Five West, to room 510. The sounds of hospital became mind-numbingly familiar: the whir of the wheels of carts, pages over the intercom, the knocks at the door. These sounds never stopped and rarely changed. Interruptions to my grading of student papers were as common as cannabis dispensaries in Oregon. From home I had brought August's boom box, and day after day I was his DJ, mixing things up with Raffi, the Muppets, and Dan Zanes. One after another I planted toys within his grasp on the bed sheets. His favorite was the Activity Atom, and as he batted at it he would emit a squeaking laugh.

Dr. Sandemelir had said that August and I would be coming into her clinic about once every six months, but now we were hunkered down in the hospital 24-7. I became what Vicki Forman in her memoir *This Lovely Life* calls "a hospital-parent specter." At the beginning of these dreary hospitalizations, I tried staying overnight, attempting to sleep on an extremely uncomfortable foldout chair. Toward midnight one night I pirated a couple of cans of Jon Boat from Jacksonville's Intuition Ale Works into August's room and hid them among his toys. I didn't think I'd get busted, but, in the darkness, a nurse unexpectedly entered and heard that unmistakable snap of a pop-top being opened. She switched on the light and then gave me a tongue-lashing worthy of a Prohibition-era teetotaler.

"Sir! This is a children's hospital!"

I quickly discovered that I could not sleep for more than forty-five minutes at a stretch, so I started driving home every night and returning to the hospital around 6:15 a.m. Ilene would spell me for a few hours whenever she could, but her fixed work schedule made her unavailable during weekdays. She also had Clio to look after, and she wouldn't have been able to lift August (due to the herniated disc in her neck), something for which I sometimes needed to be on hand. So I lived for the most part at the hospital, preparing classes and grading papers by August's bedside and only leaving to drive to campus to teach or home to sleep.

Many parents had to leave their children alone all day in their hospital rooms because they couldn't afford to miss work. If a patient was very young, nurses would pull the crib up to the room's doorway so that the little occupant could see the nurses in the corridor—and so the nurses could see the patient. With crib bars at so many doorways, the place resembled a zoo.

"This next surgery will resolve the problem." A faint Argentine accent whispered around the edges of Dr. Joyce's words. He said this several times, right before August was heading into yet another major operation. He kept insisting that he could fix things, and, on his recommendation, I kept signing consent forms for further procedures. Ilene and I didn't see any way out of this predicament. It is easy to look back now and question this course of treatment, but in the fog of war we went along. The doctor was telling us that our son needed these surgeries. To say no would have been like getting out of the endodontist's chair in the middle of a root canal procedure.

Whenever I spoke with Dr. Joyce, my voice became adenoidal, a little catch suddenly showing up in my throat. There was something paralyzing about being in the presence of this grandee of the house of medicine. One time, while waiting with August for our appointment to begin, an enthusiastic young male resident physician spoke with me. He was one of the residents among whom Joyce held court during rounds. The fellow now went on and on concerning Dr. Joyce's eminence. "It's such a privilege to work with him!" he gushed.

Some of the Bensalem-Salomon physicians were not so awestruck. A few began approaching me privately, and, speaking sotto voce, informed me that trying to save hardware compromised by infection was futile. "It rarely works," said Dr. Munodi. A few doctors took me aside individually to advise me to give up on the pump. Alexander Pope wrote, "Who shall decide when doctors disagree?"—and that question applied here. Dr. Walker was particularly emphatic: "That monstrosity of grandiosity needs to come out *now*." But Walker and Munodi were not August's regular doctors. Not only were Munodi and Walker in line with Dr. Cohen, but they also intimated that a spirited debate was taking place behind the walls of this institution—a war in heaven. Dr. Munodi told me as much. Dr. Joyce's manner of treating our son was being "hotly debated" in the hospital's medical community.

July, when the Relaxanoid pump was implanted, is the cruelest month. Ilene and I did not know this at the time, but the month can be considered cruel on account of the "July effect," an increase in the risk of medical errors and surgical complications when medical school graduates begin their residencies. In the United Kingdom, a similar phenomenon is called "the killing season." This is to say that early July is not the best time to have a major—or perhaps any—procedure performed in a teaching hospital. Dr. Joyce himself had several decades of experience, but who knows with which intern-just-turned-resident he worked? Who knows who did what with August?

Every institution has a few malcontents, so at first I assumed that the dissenting voices were coming from that small cadre. But the sub rosa dissent kept surfacing. One of the main dissenters was Dr. Munodi. One day, with the door of August's hospital room closed—it was just the three of us present—he informed me that it was his opinion that Dr. Joyce wasn't properly weighing benefit versus harm. There could be secondary effects, he warned: a number of major surgeries conducted in quick succession like August was undergoing could initiate an unintended consequence down the line. On another occasion, Munodi speculated that Joyce was trying to save August's pump because he needed to prove something to his younger colleagues, who generally didn't like him. It was obvious to me from Munodi's tone that he himself didn't. Keeping the pump in, Munodi asserted, was a matter of Joyce's pride mixed with generalized hubris.

The pediatric neurosurgery program that Dr. Joyce had founded and was running under the auspices of a local university was implanting a lot of pumps in children. A pro-pump camp and an anti-pump faction, I inferred, had formed at Bensalem-Salomon.

During one of his unsolicited visits, Dr. Munodi asked me, "Did you come under any pressure to choose the pump over other options?"

"I don't know," I said. I stood there before him in August's room, pondering and suddenly feeling dismayed. "I suppose," I hesitantly answered. I hadn't thought in such stark terms about that period when Dr. Sandemelir was advising me to switch from Botox injections to the pump.

"There has been some urgency to move pumps," he muttered disapprovingly. "The hospital's mark-up is considerable. The pumps are a profit center. The place is becoming a mill." What he said reminded me of several lines from the Dire Straits song "Money for Nothing" about "moving" consumer products. Dr. Munodi's words were an unwelcome data point.

After hearing Dr. Munodi say "move pumps," I suddenly had doubt in a way that I didn't have before. What he had said distressed me. Years later, in February 2013, *Time* magazine published Steven Brill's 24,000-word article "Bitter Pill: Why Medical Bills Are Killing Us." Brill investigated hospital billing practices and revealed that their executives were gaming the system to maximize revenue. Reading that piece, I wondered if the pump had been prescribed for ulterior purposes. It may have been the right mode of treatment, but, then again, maybe it wasn't. Did the hospital and the university promote it out of self-interest? Verifying what Dr. Munodi had asserted, Brill reported that hospitals' mark-ups for digital implanted devices (mechanisms such as the Hippocrates Relaxanoid pumps) were astronomical, serving as major sources of profit. Had Dr. Sandemelir, a university employee, been urged to recommend more of them than she otherwise would have?

Years later, in a 2014 TED Talk, "What Your Doctor Won't Disclose," Dr. Leana Wen stated that, for medicine to work, patients have to be able to trust their doctors. When the trust is gone, all that's left is fear. I now felt fear. After hearing Dr. Munodi say "move pumps," I began paying attention to the news reports about doctors being highly paid speakers for pharmaceutical and medical device companies, receiving financial incentives to prescribe this drug or that device, mainly for the purpose of lining their pockets. The Hippocrates company was often mentioned in these reports, which claimed that it used lucrative under-the-table benefits (kickbacks) such as stock options, royalty agreements, consulting agreements, research grants, and fellowships to reward doctors who prescribed its products.

As far as I had been able to tell, financial concerns never directly drove Dr. Sandemelir's or Dr. Joyce's decision-making. Being university employees, they were paid a salary and not on a fee-for-service basis. Moreover, their employer prohibited them from accepting kickbacks. On the other hand, Dr. Munodi was implying that the hospital and university administrators were operating not to personally benefit themselves but for the good of their organizations. Generally, the administrators of nonprofit and university hospitals are people in suits, businessmen and businesswomen, not doctors in white coats. For them, the institutions they run are fundamentally businesses.

Yet I didn't believe that these reports about economic incentives had anything to do with August's care. Somehow I continued to rationalize that Walker, Munodi, and Cohen were "old school" and that Joyce and Sandemelir were research scientists at medicine's cutting edge. They represented the best and the brightest. They were avatars of the future.

In any case, August's body had become the site of a proxy battle.

The operations were brutal for our son and hard on Ilene and me. Because UNF offered no paid family leave, and because Ilene and I were not able to take time off from work, we couldn't be on hand during the surgeries. So we had come to rely on Katrina Johnson, who stayed with him during the day to keep him company and to take care of him after the procedures. When we first hired her, she was a UNF student, and for about six years she worked as August's principal caregiver. She grew to love him like a brother, and August in return loved her. We considered her family, and so having her at the hospital was like one of us staying with him. Often she was the one present when he awoke from the anesthesia. In the post-surgery phases, she'd had to hold his head up as he vomited into a towel.

Six surgeries in all, each with general anesthesia, were performed over a period of four months. The first was to implant the pump. This took place on July 8, 2010. The second, third, and fourth surgeries were devoted to attempting to disinfect the device and thus prevent further infection. A fifth surgery would be performed to finally remove the pump. And then, because cerebrospinal fluid wouldn't stop leaking out of the incision site at the base of the spine, a final surgery was undertaken to address that problem. After this last one, Dr. Joyce told me that he had done "something special" to bind up August's back internally so that the oozing would stop, but he didn't elaborate much concerning what this had been.

The infection finally abated with the removal of the pump, and the discharge of cerebrospinal fluid from the incision site stopped with the sixth and final surgery, but the pump's aftereffects were like a listserv that doesn't have a button for you to unsubscribe. August had undergone five hospitalizations in few months. His number of days as an inpatient totaled more than fifty.

In late October 2010, this period in our lives came to an end. When I brought August back home for the last time, I surveyed the damage. So many operations had left his lower back a crisscross of permanent scars.

VIII

BY THE LATE SPRING OF 2011, AUGUST HAD MOSTLY recovered from the six surgeries of the preceding summer and fall, so we were able to get him back outside again in his walking device, the Rifton. Before the 2010 procedures, he had so loved walking in it. With the pump no longer inside him, we assumed that he would return to doing what he had done previously—pacing jerkily up and down the driveway. As before, he became excited when we rolled him in his wheelchair out the kitchen door, down the ramp, through the carport, and out to the top of our long driveway. As before, he squealed exuberantly as we lifted him out of the wheelchair and dropped him vertically into the Rifton. But then, once inside the device, he made no attempt to walk. He just stood there. This was the way things became for him. Permanently. Just standing still. He now was like a statue, a happy stationary fixture cooing in the wind. Gone forever were the days of fevered striding and the jollity of adventure.

Also, and exponentially more serious than not walking, was something incredibly creepy that had started occurring several months earlier, in November 2010, less than thirty days following the last of Dr. Joyce's six surgeries. This was behavior Ilene and I had never witnessed. Dr. Munodi had warned that Joyce wasn't properly weighing benefit versus harm and that there could be unwanted secondary effects. And this indeed came to pass.

August had begun arching. Arching, also known as extension, meant that, for periods lasting for up to ten days, August would involuntarily bend backward and to the side in a twisted position and remain in it. His limbs would be distorted, his back bent, as if perpetually trying to glance over his shoulder at his heels, causing him to resemble a human pretzel. For days on end he would be stuck in this contortion. In ballet, there is a pose called *attitude derrière*, and August sort of looked like that except that his leg wouldn't be up in midair, his head would be permanently cocked to the side, and he couldn't get out of it. "Fixity of posture and muscular rigidity" was how this condition was clinically described. External stimuli didn't seem to bring on an episode, so we had no idea what event, if any, would trigger one. For the next three years, arching became, like Russia for Winston Churchill, a "riddle wrapped in a mystery inside an enigma."

During these recurring ten-day periods, it was as if a monstrous winged reptile were roosting atop our house. This was an enormous, shrieking bird from one million BC, a pterodactyl unlike the blithe variety we had known. This one was ominous and fearsome. Ilene and I experienced constant anxiety on account of it. If we weren't dealing with its presence, we were anticipating its return. For perhaps fourteen days August would be his usual, relaxed, calm self, but then something inexplicable would trigger an episode. The first sign of it would be a brief, involuntary gesture, a jerk, a twist, an arm spasm, something we named "the Egyptian." The Egyptian would consist of his left arm suddenly shooting out as in a stock image of an ancient Egyptian. It would be a momentary gesture, but it would be enough to let me know that the dreaded prehistoric bird had appeared again on the western horizon and was rapidly winging its way toward us.

The Egyptian would be followed by three to five days of gradual ramping up, of August's ever-increasing inability to sleep, and more and more nervous, manic behavior. Then, following this build-up, for perhaps the next five to seven days, he would remain in a fixed, twisted posture, stiff as a board, the Full Pterodactyl. Ancient, even primordial, it was a locked-in-a-pretzel form in which August would remain petrified for days. During the Full Pterodactyl, he would go for forty, fifty, even sixty hours straight without sleeping.

From the way he pursed his lips during the Full Pterodactyl I knew that August was uncomfortable. All of his life I had argued to others—mainly to disability skeptics who automatically assumed that he must be living in torment and so should be taken out of his misery—that August wasn't suffering. And he hadn't been. But during these arching episodes I had to admit that he was going through pain and distress. It was not constant, but there were hours during which he would moan and groan. And then the Full Pterodactyl would slowly subside. Afterward he would experience a period of calm lasting for as long as two weeks.

People who say that God doesn't send you anything you can't handle have never encountered a situation like this. With each lengthy arching attack, August's condition would be so horrible to behold, so awful and appalling, that it would become almost impossible for me to bear. In the morning I would become afraid to go into his room to perform his daily hygiene. My hand lingering on the doorknob, I would listen to his moaning and visualize his lips pursed, face wan, and body pretzelized. The mere thought of August's hideously twisted shape would sweep me up like gale-force winds and carry me away. I wanted to escape, to move to some other state, to be some other person. But I was his father, so I would push through the dread and do my job. I would turn the knob and bound into the room and screech at him at the top of my lungs in the same Wicked Witch of the West voice that I'd always used to herald August's day. Twisted as he would be, the little performance would still amuse him. And this, for a moment at least, would be the eye of the hurricane.

No one at Bensalem-Salomon had any idea what the problem was. Every doctor who weighed in on the matter did so from the perspective of his or her specialty. The gastro-enterologist was the GERD Man. Whatever the symptoms or the question, his answer always seemed to be "GERD" (gastroesophageal reflux disease). The orthopedist suggested the extreme solution of "rodding"—inserting titanium rods into August's crooked back to keep it straight. To his credit, this doctor, who I knew to be caring and conscientious, indicated through his body language that even he thought that this was a terrible idea. "I'm sorry," he said, "but I just don't have any other tools in my tool kit."

Did the Full Pterodactyl emerge from the succession of six operations August had undergone over four months? Did it come from something undertaken in the last of them? The fifth surgery had removed the pump, but cerebrospinal fluid had continued oozing from the incision site at the base of the spine. So, Dr. Joyce had performed the sixth and last to stop the leak. Afterward, he had told me that he'd done something special to get the job done. There was a seal, a patch of some kind. But he must have patched the site of the leak too tightly because nothing resembling arching had occurred prior to that last surgery, and it started less than a month afterward. The facts pointed in that direction.

Ilene and I racked our brains trying to figure out what had brought on the arching. Did the sixth surgery inadvertently inflict neurological damage? Was any part of a bone in the spinal column removed, leaving a sharp edge? Or did the surgery cause scar tissue to form in or around the spinal cord? Or, in tightening the dura, did Dr. Joyce overdo it, inadvertently creating a tethered cord?

Perhaps a second Relaxanoid pump would help by subduing the arching. For the few months in the summer and fall of 2010 when August had the pump in his body, we had seen the device doing exactly what it was supposed to do, relieve spasticity. In and of itself, the device was effective. So I speculated that implanting another might address the arching. Dr. Sandemelir agreed that, indeed, another pump might address the problem and so was willing to have a second one put in.

Dr. Cohen again attempted to dissuade me. As I expected, he was adamant. One year following the last set of surgeries, he insisted, was not enough time for August's body to fully recover. He needed more rest before another major surgery. This time I disregarded Cohen's advice for a different reason than before: Ilene and I now were beside ourselves, sick with worry, almost frantic. By this time we had returned to the regimen of Botox injections and oral Relaxanoid, but they did nothing to relieve the arching, which had become an overwhelming problem driving us to distraction. Dr. Sandemelir advised us that another Relaxanoid pump might help. She didn't promise that the pump would stop the arching, but she didn't dissuade us from thinking that it might. We asked for a different doctor in the pediatric neurosurgery program to implant the second one, and, in the summer of 2011, a neurosurgeon much younger than Dr. Joyce, Dr. Tom Gordon, did so. The Yellow Man was on hand once again, monitoring the situation, present in the operating room, but I didn't speak with him.

No infection occurred this time, and, somewhat surprisingly, by January 2012 our son was back for brief periods in his Rifton, standing at the top of the driveway in the shade of a small oak tree. Now August had the pump inside him without us having to worry about infection, so we could see what it could do. But as had started happening the year before with the first pump, August just stood in his Rifton, not attempting to move. Was the amount of Relaxanoid the pump was dispensing into his system the correct dose? Was it too high? Too low? If August had been verbal, he might have been able to help by telling us what he was feeling. Dr. Sandemelir had assured me that she intended to rely on clinical observation to determine the right dose. But August was a black box, a Neil Armstrong without radio communication.

By this point the golden visions that Dr. Sandemelir had conjured up when first pitching the pump to us had vanished. She had suggested not only that August would walk more gracefully but also that he might be able to feed himself. But with the second pump, attempts to help him do the latter made no progress. After a number of months of working with him, the occupational therapists at Mt. Herman told me that the pump had done absolutely nothing to improve his prospects. No possibility in the foreseeable future existed that he would be able to feed himself.

Ilene and I had requested the second Relaxanoid pump to be implanted to address the arching, but we found that it did nothing to alleviate that. August's cycles of arching actually accelerated. But the pump did one thing well: it relieved August of charley horses. With the second pump, not once did he push up from his wheelchair's foot pedals and scream out as he had done much earlier. This indeed was a benefit, but it was one that could also have been achieved by using small doses of oral Relaxanoid together with Botox injections.

One time while an arching episode coincided with a clinic visit, Dr. Sandemelir looked over August as he lay pretzeled on her exam table. She said that she had no idea what was causing the arching and no insight concerning what to do. Never did she indicate that this phenomenon had a name, and she acted as if she had never seen it before. But what was most troubling was that she exhibited minimal curiosity about it.

"I can't find any fault with the pump," she said reassuringly during one of August's visits to her clinic. "It's functioning as it should."

"You don't think it might have something to do with the arching?" I said.

"No, not really. The pump is not implicated."

Her job, she intimated, was simply to manage the Relaxanoid pump, nothing more. From her vantage point, the device was functioning perfectly well, and that was all that mattered. We should find some other doctor to deal with the arching, she advised, and she recommended that we see a neurologist. The neurologist we had once met with in Bensalem-Salomon was hopelessly disability-phobic, so we couldn't go to him. Observing August, Dr. Sandemelir sighed and said, "I wish I was smarter."

During subsequent visits to her clinic I brought the matter up again and again. I was doing this more frequently because the arching was worsening.

"If you are not happy with the pump," she said once, "we can remove it."

"I'm not unhappy with the pump," I replied. "I'm unhappy with the arching. It's making his life and ours unbearable."

"As I've said, the pump is not implicated in the arching." Her tone was pleasant but defensive.

But then, in the middle of 2012, Dr. Sandemelir and her physician assistant, Ms. Bosman, began to suspect that perhaps the pump catheter was leaking or damaged or kinking and that maybe one of these had something to do with the arching. Yet another major surgery was scheduled, a procedure known as a catheter revision. It would replace not the pump itself but only the catheter. This was the line that went from the pump on the side of August's lower belly around his body to the base of spinal column and then upward to a point about midway up his back. So, on the morning of August 1, 2012—Ilene's and my twentieth wedding anniversary—Dr. Gordon undertook the procedure.

In the evening after the catheter-revision surgery, Ilene and I had just enough time to meet for glasses of champagne and salads at Bistro Aix, a trendy restaurant. She had found someone to watch Clio for a couple of hours. Not even having had a chance to change clothes, I bought a small bouquet at the hospital gift shop.

We sat at the bar because we were rushed: I had to get back to August's bedside. The celebration would last just twenty minutes, one minute for each of our twenty years. There was a couple seated to our left, probably in their early

twenties. I saw that the guy was wearing a Dead Kennedys–
Holiday in Cambodia T-shirt. This was another madeleine
dipped in tea and caused me to reflect, *He could have been me
thirty years ago.*

From where we were positioned we could see the restaurant kitchen, noisy but fun to watch. Our waiter—a tall,
skinny, well-inked fellow with a serious set of ear gauges—
took our orders: glasses of 2008 Schramsberg Extra Brut, a
small calamari salad for me, and an heirloom beet salad for
her. We told the waiter that I needed to hurry, to get back
to the hospital. He nodded approvingly, probably assuming
that I was a doctor who would tip him well.

We had honeymooned for a week in the Napa wine
country, where we visited, among many places, Schramsberg. After our glasses of sparkling wine arrived, we sat for
a moment contemplating them, watching the bubbles rise.

"Whoever would have thought we'd be celebrating our
twentieth with a child in the hospital," I said.

"I would never have imagined it," Ilene said.

"So here's to the best twenty years of my life," I said as I
raised my glass.

"And here's to the best twenty years of my life," she said,
raising hers.

"And may we have at least twenty more good years."

"At least twenty."

"L'chaim!" I said as we clinked our champagne glasses
together.

"L'chaim!"

And we sipped our drinks.

"Do you remember Our Song?" said Ilene. "'Losing My
Religion'?"

"R.E.M. Of course. It's been a long time. 'Oh, life is bigger,' I sang, the opening line.

"No, that's not how the song begins," she corrected. "It's 'O life! It's bigger.'"

"I really don't think so," I countered. "It starts with an 'Oh.'"

"No, there's no 'Oh.' Just 'O.' There's no *h*. Seriously! There's just 'O.' A vocative *O*, the *O* when addressing someone, as in 'O ye, of little faith.' The song goes, 'O life! It's bigger—.'"

"No way," I said. "It's got to be an *Oh*. *Oh* is an interjection, and the singer is using it to express his pain, surprise, frustration, and disappointment. It's '*Oooohhhhhh*, life is bigger.' The song's about unrequited love. The person he's speaking to doesn't love him back, but he's saying to her—I assume it's a her—it could be a him—that it doesn't matter, that life is bigger than that person's love. It's really about sour grapes. It's a the-fact-that-you-are-not-loving-me-back-is-not-important-to-*me* argument. And love itself is not that important. It's like the circles in a Venn diagram. Life overlaps and covers over most of the smaller one, love."

Ilene thought about this for a moment and then shot back, "But the relative sizes of the circles in your Venn diagram are inverted. Because it's *O*, love's the bigger circle. It overlaps and covers over most of the smaller one, life. If the line is, 'O life! It's bigger,' then the point is, the love circle is bigger, not the other way around. Love is all, or almost all. That's why he's saying, 'O life! It's bigger.' 'It' here equals love, and love is bigger than life."

"I'm not convinced. Love may be big, but it's not *that* big." The thought struck me that this was not the thing to be saying at an anniversary dinner. "And then in the next line he sings, 'It's bigger than you and me,' meaning that life is bigger than both himself and the other person combined. In other words, life is bigger than love. It's bigger than you and I. He's basically saying, 'I don't need you.'"

"You're wrong there!" she announced exultantly. "That's not even the second line. The next line goes, 'It's bigger than you and you are not me.'"

Hmmm. Was this true? We pulled out our iPhones, and the lyric sheets we found online confirmed that her version indeed was the second line. But as for the first, the lyric sheets were no help.

Because of August and his medical needs, this had become the central question of our marriage: Will life be bigger than love? Or will love be bigger than life? Which in the end would triumph?

IX

A CHANGE WAS MADE WITHOUT OUR PERMISSION. Before the catheter-revision surgery, the tip of the catheter in August had stopped midway up the thoracic spine. After the surgery, it terminated in a new location, one much higher. Dr. Sandemelir had instructed the neurosurgeon, Dr. Gordon, to raise the tip to the second cervical vertebrae, C2, right below the skull. This was supposed to allow the benefits of Relaxanoid to be distributed throughout the greatest extent of August's body.

Dr. Sandemelir hadn't asked for our consent for this change. She didn't inform me until the day after the surgery, so I hadn't known about it during Ilene's and my anniversary celebration. When Sandemelir told me, I didn't think much about it. But when I mentioned it during one of my frequent cell phone updates to Ilene, she became livid. She didn't like not having been consulted, she would never have approved, and she feared that it would lead to a terrible consequence.

And that is indeed what happened. A few days later I brought August home from the hospital, and, as Ilene had predicted, the unthinkable occurred—what had been very bad became even worse. August's arching suddenly, dramatically, astronomically increased to a new level of wretchedness. Overnight it became orders of magnitude greater, going from simple nightmare into the deepest realm of the macabre. August's reaction went well beyond the dreaded Full Pterodactyl. What had been mere arching became arching in extremis. Like some figure out of Ovid, our son had metamorphosed into a twisted tree trunk of a boy, wrapping around himself, all kinks and swirls.

Fear gripped me. August's neck had become so bent that he couldn't take anything by mouth—I had no way of getting food or drink into him. Whatever he did swallow he immediately projectile-vomited, something he'd never done before. In the state he was in, he was going to starve to death. And, on top of everything, he was crying, crying, crying. At my wits' end and terrified, I decided to take him to the ER. His torso was so deformed, though, that I could barely strap him into his wheelchair. Once I finally managed to do that, I drove him to Bensalem-Salomon.

The next morning at about eleven, Dr. Sandemelir came over from her clinic to August's hospital room. She blew through the door like a bitter northern wind. She was alone— the Yellow Man did not accompany her, nor did Dr. Joyce. At the beginning of their intervention, in 2010, these three had been all over August's case, but now, in 2012, they were fading from view.

Samuel Johnson writes, "There are a thousand familiar disputes, which reason can never decide." This sentiment applied here, for from the start she was incredulous and defensive, openly doubting me when I told her that the arching had intensified. She moved around August's bed, tapping his knees and feet, seeking reflexes. She wouldn't make eye contact with or engage with me.

"But *why* do you believe the extension has increased?" she finally asked, her tone short and dismissive.

"Because it has," I said, confounded by her question. "I can tell by looking at him. Can't you? By trying to feed him. By trying to get him to drink."

She didn't say anything as she continued to check his reflexes.

"Why would I be making this up?" I asked, staring at her averted face. My question hung in the air. I could see that she was a young physician trying to handle a difficult situation. I knew that she was bright and dedicated and that she wanted to do what was best, but I also was beginning to see that she suffered from tunnel vision.

She had ceased checking August's reflexes and was standing motionless on one side of his bed, I on the other. Below and between us lay August's perversely twisted form, a vision straight out of the book of Revelation. She again bent over the bed and began to manipulate his limbs, checking his range of motion. As she touched him, he made no sound, and his angelic face was expressionless. She couldn't manipulate his left arm because it had an IV. And there was another line: a feeding tube had been inserted into his nostril, down the esophagus, and into his stomach.

As she tested his legs she repeated calmly that no connection could exist between the catheter revision surgery and the arching, which, anyway, she doubted had gotten worse.

"It has gotten worse," I insisted, my voice rising. "Infinitely worse. It came from the catheter revision surgery."

She looked up and finally met my gaze, squinting at me. She appeared offended by what I'd said. "That's not possible," she announced, shaking her head.

"If it wasn't the catheter revision surgery causing it," I said, flummoxed, "then why is this happening now, right after the surgery?"

She repeated that the catheter revision "couldn't possibly" be implicated.

"Then explain to me why," I said, "that just three days after this last surgery, he's arching more than ever. He can't eat or drink. How am I going to feed him?"

"We—," she began. But then she suddenly lost momentum. She stopped speaking and moving. Perhaps the fact that August couldn't take any liquid or food by mouth had finally sunk in. She glanced over her left shoulder at the closed hospital room door. Was she, like the sorcerer's apprentice, wishing that some older physician like Dr. Joyce—a wise old sorcerer—would enter, take over, set things right, make the floodwaters abate? No one came. There was only stillness and silence. Then she looked down but not particularly at August, and for several moments she appeared to be reevaluating the situation.

"He can't even eat now," I said, much more gently than before. "I need to know what to do. I need to know why."

She had lost her fizz. And then, almost as if she needed to find something to do to keep her hands busy, she leaned over the bed railing and again examined August's grotesquely convoluted body. She was not looking at me as she fidgeted. She finally conceded, in a low voice I could barely hear, "I don't know why."

In retrospect, I realize that she was caught in the mind trap of local suboptimization, a concept that originated in the business world. The *Oxford English Dictionary* defines *suboptimization* as "the optimizing of an individual part or department within an organization, rather than the organization as a whole." Economist Thayer Watkins says that the term "has been adopted for a common policy mistake. It refers to the practice of focusing on one component of a total and making changes intended to improve that one component and ignoring the effects on the other components." Watkins illustrates with this example: "a firm focuses on minimization [of] cost . . . and takes measures which not only reduce cost but also reduce revenues." To a much smaller degree, the term *local suboptimization* has been used in scientific circles. I first heard the phrase while listening to Ira Flatow's NPR program, *Science Friday.* In science, it describes a situation in which a scientist can see what is correct but only within a very small frame. He or she understands what is true within a tiny space but cannot take into account the bigger contextual picture. In medicine, the term has hardly been used at all outside of the field of hospital organizational management. Local suboptimization applied to Dr. Sandemelir's case to the extent that she saw that the pump was working well, and this was all that mattered to her.

Day after day August lay in his hospital bed like a contortionist unable to find the way back to his starting posture. The arching just wouldn't abate, and I thought, *Quoth the pterodactyl, "Nevermore."* I began recycling scenes from August's birth, as though that event in 1999 and this 2012 episode had blended together to form one continuous violation. In my mind, I shouted accusations that had roots in events thirteen years earlier. Someone monitoring my thoughts would have concluded that I was becoming unhinged.

Dr. Sandemelir finally suggested turning up the flow of Relaxanoid to solve the arching. "This may help," she said one day. And so the flow rate was gradually increased over several weeks' time but without positive result.

"Ah, August," Dr. Sandemelir mumbled on several occasions, shaking her head, as though he was being a very bad boy for not going along with the program. She may not have intended to, but she was blaming the patient.

In the fall of 2012 August and I were living again on Five West, once more in room 510. It felt as though the fall of 2010 had never ceased. We were back in the implacable routine of hospitals. Everything from two years earlier flooded back: the rhythms of hospital life; the bells, beeps, and intercom pages; the sound of wheels and knocks at the door; the odors of physicality. Seeing that August and I had returned, one of the nurses joked, "You better not try and escape."

During this stay August tested positive for MRSA (methicillin-resistant Staphylococcus aureus). Doctors and nurses this time treated him with extreme caution. Everyone coming into his hospital room had to scrub up and wear a special yellow paper gown and then wash again before leaving the room. The intention behind these special procedures was to reduce the risk of August's MRSA spreading and becoming some other patient's hospital-generated disease. I found these precautions confusing. They would have made perfect sense two years earlier but didn't at this time, when arching was the issue and no sign of infection was evident. Still, I went along willingly because I understood that the hospital was trying to do the right thing.

August spent his days in bed and was turned periodically to prevent bedsores. Beneath him a thin but active electric air mattress hummed. The railings on each side always remained raised to prevent him from tumbling out. Small electronic monitors perched gargoyle-like above him, and they displayed colorful, squiggly, moving lines. These announced his rates of heartbeat and oxygenation, the metrics of his helpless little being. At least once every hour or two the electrodes attached to his body or the pulse oximeter gripping his finger would loosen. A noisy beeping would ensue and not be silenced until a nurse came, and sometimes that would take as long as fifteen minutes. Occasionally the monitors would go off for no apparent reason, to the same effect—a long wait for a nurse to quell the beeping.

August spent sixty-four straight days in Bensalem-Salomon. We couldn't find our way to the exit. Every day was a roller coaster of emotions, highs and lows, creating endless nervous stress. During this period August and I communicated in our own special language, and we listened to each other's silences. But as the weeks dragged on, the wordless speech ran dry. Of the two of us, at least he remained cheerful.

At times August was in tremendous discomfort. He howled for hours in pain. Once he bellowed all night. So loudly did he do so that I could hear him from the far end of the corridor. It was late, and I had just come back from eating dinner in the cafeteria on the ground level. After I exited the elevator and entered Five West, I could hear him. He was far away. Between where he lay and where I stood were many hospital-room doors. All of them were shut. Immediately I knew who it was.

During the day, Bensalem-Salomon clinicians trooped in to have a look: wave after wave of white walkers. Inquisitive faces would approach the subject in his bed and peer down. Not one knew what to say. Not one suggested a name for August's condition. Not one seemed to have the slightest clue why he was arching. All appeared mystified. But most importantly, no one believed that what August was enduring was his or her problem to solve.

Memories of two in particular stayed with me. One was a young, bantering male clinician, who said with witty aplomb, "Wow! That can't be comfortable." He delivered this wisecrack while viewing my boy all balled up in a knot. The other was a raven-haired young female physician, who chided, "What is wrong with you!? You are a parent in denial!" Wagging her finger, she sharply informed me that I was a parent unable to come to terms with the fact that my child was "suffering from cerebral palsy."

During these physicians' visits, August was having trouble keeping food in his tummy. The feeding tube wasn't entirely doing the trick, and his weight—never ideally high—was declining.

Neither Dr. Walker nor Dr. Munodi came by. I don't know where they went, but they didn't seem to be at the hospital anymore. Dr. Joyce was still running the pediatric neurosurgery program, but I had no desire to speak with him.

Being caught in the health-care system is like being caught in the legal system, especially if it is regarding a child. Once the bureaucracy ensnares you, you can't simply walk away. You must play by its rules. So August and I were, as Doron Weber says of himself and his son Damon in his 2012 book *Immortal Bird*, "doing hard time in the bowels of American medicine."

The hospital's operation was shambolic. Each clinician who August and I dealt with was functioning on his or her own—cowboy style—consulting with other physicians only on an ad hoc basis. It was wormhole thinking. Each approached August's case through the eyes of his or her specialty; each was in a silo, separate from the others, and each had the one-tool approach that comes with specialties, so that, overall, August's care was fragmented. It was as if they had all had collectively decided to turn the field of medicine into a massive medieval passion play re-creating the Tower of Babel.

I had always looked favorably on palliative care doctors. Only a truly sensitive and caring person, I assumed, would take up such a specialty. And I still believe this. I would wager as an uneducated guess that over 95 percent of them are genuinely good, caring, sensitive people because it takes a special type of person to do that kind of work. But, as it happened, we ran into one of the few bad apples. Dr. Kim Eugenides seemed to have an agenda all her own. The first time she entered August's hospital room, her mind was already made up. Even before reading his chart, she knew what to do. Within minutes she began lecturing me as though from a script.

"Have you begun to think about the next phase of his life?" Standing in her white lab coat, she intimated that I should start picking out a coffin. This question's practiced quality indicated that she asked it a lot. A clinician with magical powers, she then got out her pad and started scribbling prescriptions. This physician was promiscuous with the prescription pad. These were pharmacy orders for dark potions and soporific elixirs. The Eugenides cocktail consisted of morphine, clonidine, Hycet (hydrocodone-acetaminophen), Neurontin (gabapentin), and Valium (diazepam), all to be started at once and together. Eventually, without subtracting any of these, and without explaining why, she added methadone.

The massive drugging did nothing to alleviate the arching, which was the problem that needed solving. Her potions didn't do anything except keep August "snowed." It couldn't have been pleasant. And sometimes there were paradoxical responses in which, instead of being sleepy, he became agitated. But most importantly, the more the doctor drugged him, the more a chain reaction set in. One by one the physicians at Bensalem-Salomon stepped back and checked out. If Dr. Eugenides had been called in and was giving August a maximum of drugs, he must be dying. To my mind, Dr. Eugenides's drug regimen was the most idiotic aspect of August's treatment at Bensalem-Salomon.

Like the other physicians, Dr. Paul Sticks, who lived in our San Marco neighborhood, wasn't able to solve the arching riddle. August was noisily playing with a toy when Dr. Sticks came into his room. Speaking slowly, Sticks said that Ilene and I should figure out what our end-of-life wishes would be for August. What would we want the hospital to do if a life-threatening situation arose and one of us was not present?

"Life and death," I said.

He looked at me sympathetically but did not speak.

"What life, what death?" I said.

"It would be good for us to know what the wishes of the parents are."

Our wishes? Wasn't this topic premature? How could death be the topic when the patient was busy thrashing his toy? I couldn't wrap my mind around the two ideas at once: August playing, August dying. The two ideas were incongruous. Once the subject had been broached, however, Ilene and I had to follow through. We wanted to be responsible parents. What *would* we want the hospital to do? Very late that night, we discussed the matter. Given our schedules, even this conversation had to be rushed, and we held it while brushing our teeth.

Central to our decision, when we reached one, was the wish that August not suffer. A feeding tube was one thing, acceptable in the big scheme of things, but a ventilator was quite another. We did not want him to be put on one, not if there would be little chance of him ever coming off it. We didn't want him to endure pain by being kept alive if the only reason for sustaining his life was that we couldn't let go of him.

The following day, before he went off shift, Dr. Sticks helped us put our names to a "do not resuscitate" (DNR) order. (This directive has since been renamed an AND— "allow natural death.") Ilene and I met with him in the late afternoon. We hovered and agonized over the document.

"I want to make certain," Ilene said, holding the pen, "that August will continue to receive the same level of care he is receiving now."

"He will," said Dr. Sticks.

"If signing this form means there's going to be a change in his status or a drop off in his care in any way, I don't want to sign," she said. "Will he be treated the same?"

"Yes," Dr. Sticks assured her. "His status will remain the same. He won't be treated any differently just because you have signed a DNR."

Ilene hesitated for a long time, mulling it over. Finally she said, "Okay then. If nothing is going to change. We're only signing this document in the event of the worst of a worst-case scenario. I don't want the doctors or the nurses or the staff or anyone to lessen their care because we've signed this form. We believe that he will recover if he is given proper care."

"Nothing will change," said Dr. Sticks reassuringly.

So she signed it. And I did too. And we had copies made to take home with us. This DNR order became like the handle on an airliner's emergency exit door. We didn't expect to ever have to use it.

But August's de facto status did change. It was a subtle difference. It was as if his hospital room had sprung a slow leak of oxygen. In the same way that everyone interpreted Dr. Eugenides's intervention to mean that August's end was nigh, so it was with the DNR. This was especially true of the nurses. The DNR apparently depressed them—they seemed more somber knowing that it was in his chart. The nurses emotionally stepped back, preparing themselves for the worst. And I don't blame them—the deaths of children are hard on them. No one wants to see a child die.

As if pulling us back from the brink, a gastroenterologist, Dr. Nassar, hypothesized that August might be suffering from superior mesenteric artery syndrome (or SMA). This was what may have been causing the arching. Not all of the doctors concerned with August's care accepted Nassar's diagnosis, but, lacking any better one, they more or less went along and began treating him for it. SMA is rare and extremely serious. Up to one-third of SMA patients die as a result of it. We fully understood at this moment that August's life was in danger. SMA treatment required the patient to gain weight, specifically, in August's case, to build up fat deposits in his lower stomach area.

The hospital's main pediatric surgeon, Dr. Sherwood, surgically implanted a G-J (gastrostomy-jejunostomy) tube so that August's amount of nutrition could be increased. When he opened August up to implant the G-J tube, what he saw inside convinced him that Dr. Nassar's SMA diagnosis was valid. Because such matters were in his wheelhouse,

I believed him, and I think he made the best call he could have made. Sherwood trusted me with his personal cell number and took my calls when I needed to speak with him. His own child had spent months in this same hospital, and the way he acted toward Ilene and me indicated that he understood what we were going through. He represented Bensalem-Salomon at its best.

August became wedded to a machine: he required continuous enteral feeding. An artificial opening had been created at his abdomen. This opening had two ports, the G-port (for medications going to his stomach) and the J-port (for nutrition—PediaSure—going to his jejunum, the middle part of the small intestine). We had to stay focused: medication went into the G-tube, liquid nutrition into the J-tube. Mixing this up would bring serious consequences.

Most of the day and into the night, August had to be fed this way. Every few seconds, a pump would inject a spurt of PediaSure through a transparent plastic tube to the J-port and then into the jejunum. This was called J-tube feeding. A small blue-and-white pump called a Kangaroo was the injecting mechanism. Slightly smaller than a brick, it attached midway up on an IV pole. With this nearly around-the-clock feeding, the sound of the little blue pump turning on and off every few seconds, with a several-second delay between each burst, was like white noise broken up by a predictable ripple. *Hummmmmmmm-click-grrrr! Hummmmmmmm-click-grrrr! Hummmmmmmm-click-grrrrr!* This sequence of sounds provided a constant and hypnotizing rhythm to our lives.

On an October night while August was recovering, I sat beside his hospital bed, eyes glued to a TV set projecting from an arm high on the wall, watching Barack Obama debate Mitt Romney. Other nights that month I watched the San Francisco Giants sweep the Detroit Tigers in four games in the World Series. I thought of my dad and what joy this victory would have brought him. As with the presidential debates, so it was with the World Series: the little Kangaroo pump supplied the background clicking and whirring, constant electronic music in monotones.

Since August didn't need to remain in Bensalem-Salomon for the treatment to proceed, we brought him home, fed him night and day using the Kangaroo pump, put weight on him, kept in touch with his doctors, and hoped for the best.

Once August was back home, Ilene and I found ourselves again running a home hospital. It was as if we had become triage nurses. No one at Bensalem-Salomon had suggested to Ilene and me that we should apply for home nursing.

Translucent plastic bags of PediaSure hung like ripening fruit from an adjustable transfusion pole. At night, the bags glowed like faces. The pump—with its rhythmic clicks and whirrs—operated night and day, a toiling midget. And the suction device (to clear August's airway) lay ready at hand.

To keep track of feeding and medicating, we had to chart each step every hour of the day. This was our guide seven days a week, and this went on for weeks and months and then a year. Ilene and I quickly became exhausted. We were working our regular full-time jobs, raising Clio, and taking care of a very sick child. We could not afford for either of us to stop working: because of August's medical needs, the wolf was always at our door.

By early December 2012, August had gained a lot of weight, which was the purpose of the Kangaroo pump and the incessant J-tube feeding. We had been told that if he built up fat deposits just below the stomach, then, in all likelihood, the arching should cease. And if the arching went away, he could resume feeding by mouth rather than through a J-tube. We could go back to living the life we had been enjoying up to July 7, 2010, the day before the first Relaxanoid pump was implanted. Happy days would return.

But in the middle of that month, the Egyptian showed up again, followed by the shrieking bird from one million BC flying toward us from the west. When it arrived, it circled the house several times before landing on the roof.

The massive doses of pain medication that Dr. Eugenides was prescribing accomplished nothing. But more importantly, this latest episode of the Full Pterodactyl ruled out Dr. Nassar's SMA diagnosis, the one that Dr. Sherwood thought he had verified. Whatever its cause, the arching wasn't brought on by SMA.

No explanation for the arching remained. None of the medical professionals had a clue. For almost three years, we had shown August in his state of extension to an array of doctors at Bensalem-Salomon. Now Ilene and I were back to square one. And we were alone. We acutely felt the accuracy of item fifteen on Roy Ellis's *30 Signs You May Have a Disabled Child*: "It dawns on you one day you know more than your doctor."

One particularly bad night during the December relapse, August was so extended that Ilene and I could hardly change his poopy diaper, even with the two of us working together. He was stiff and twisted, like a big piece of driftwood. Afterward, as I was lying in bed, a thought struck me. At 3 a.m. I got up and padded as quietly as I could through our house of creaking floors. I turned on the computer and sent an email to Dr. Sandemelir, telling her that we wanted her to turn off the Relaxanoid pump to see if *that* might help. It was counterintuitive, but perhaps diminishing the dose of Relaxanoid to nothing might relieve the arching. There was nothing else left. Stopping treatment—we should try that! Up until then, no one had suggested or even thought of turning the pump off.

The next morning, I drove August to Dr. Sandemelir's clinic, and we started turning down the flow of Relaxanoid. This reduction had to be accomplished over a period of many weeks, otherwise August would go into withdrawal. Ilene and I also began weaning him off the magic potions that Dr. Eugenides had ordered. Eventually we managed to take August off all of the drugs. By late February 2013, the elixirs were leaving his system, and the pump was administering only about one-third its former dose of Relaxanoid. We observed *clonus*, or shaky legs (involuntary, rhythmic, muscular contractions), return, but the cramping—the charley horses—didn't. But we still couldn't go back to feeding August by mouth, which is what we were aiming to do. We were stuck now feeding him through a J-tube, using the little blue Kangaroo pump day and night. He had to be tied to this machine almost all of the time.

As August became drug-free, his lively little personality reawakened. It was as though he had been living within a shroud, but now it had been torn open, and we could see his little cheery face inside. During this period, our goal was to return him to the relatively healthy state he'd enjoyed up to July 7, 2010. Progress or regress was measured by how far or near we were to getting him to eat food by mouth and by how near or far we were to the Nevermore Pterodactyl departing forever.

Turning down the speed of the pump and thereby lowering the dose of Relaxanoid seemed to help. Over time we became cautiously optimistic. And then we became more optimistic. And then a little more. No Egyptian, no Full Pterodactyl appeared. *We're out of the woods!* was a thought that Ilene and I began to entertain.

About this time, I started noticing hair developing on August's body. Fuzz was appearing on his upper lip. I remembered Ronnie, August's friend, the young man I'd met eight years earlier at the 2005 Spirit of the ADA march. I also sadly recalled that Ronnie was no longer alive. August's body was becoming like a man's. His shoulders were broadening, his jaw was becoming more defined, and his Adam's apple was more protruding.

Then it returned. It was a long hiatus, the longest of any up until that time. But in the spring of 2013, the Egyptian appeared, and then, a few days later, the flying reptile was back, the Full Pterodactyl. When she saw him arching for the first time in a long time, Katrina burst into tears.

The cycle of the shrieking creature again went into full swing. When the ancient bird was upon us, it screeched all day, and at night it slept on the roof. After a week or nine days, the sound of its leathery wings could be heard as it flew back toward the western horizon. We would be free again—until the next visit a few weeks later.

One afternoon Ilene broke down in tears while speaking on the phone with a caseworker. She was at the end of her rope. Fortunately, the woman on the other end of the line realized that we were a family in distress. Wheels turned, and this woman helped set us up with a home-nursing agency. Evidently, we now qualified for home nursing.

The young, fresh-faced representatives of the for-profit home-care agency who came to our house promised us the moon. When the promises weren't fulfilled and we called, we were told that these representatives had been transferred to an office in a distant city. Nurses were in our house now from eight to twelve hours a day—that is, if they showed up for work. Unlike our regular college-age caregivers at the time, Amber, Katrina, and Jobeth, they were strangers to us. The younger ones were immature and uninterested. They were nurses who, for the most part, and for whatever reason, couldn't get hired at a hospital or convalescent home. Almost all of them were trying to find more permanent positions or transitioning to move somewhere else. All of them had only two years of nursing training (AA degrees) at community colleges. The turnover was great. We would be working with one nurse (in the rotation) for a few weeks, and then, without warning, someone new would show up in her place (always a *her*). With each unexpected replacement, I would have to take an hour out of an already busy schedule to orient the new person to the job.

These home-care nurses were prone to make mistakes. Several confused what went into the G-tube (medications) with what went into the J-tube (PediaSure). I had to keep a close eye on each nurse. I will never forget the one who set the Kangaroo at a pace to pump PediaSure into August at ten times the proper rate. I still shudder when I think about it. Who knows what would have happened if I hadn't caught her mistake in time.

In "The Learning Curve," a 2002 article in the *New Yorker*, Atul Gawande writes about the need for medical organizations to sometimes test ethical limits when training tomorrow's doctors or working out the kinks of new, potentially life-saving procedures. Similarly, when a new program is getting off the ground, it often has to lower its standards in order to enroll enough patients so that it can run. Ilene had seen this happen at Loma Prieta when she was working there. The medical center had inaugurated a heart-transplant program and had taken in patients who shouldn't have been in it, people with histories of drug or alcohol abuse or other compromised conditions who died post-surgery. Dr. Joyce's pump program had to start from scratch and operate in a related, somewhat "sketchy" way in its first years until it was fully on its feet.

On the morning of Monday, October 14, 2013, August was back in Bensalem-Salomon due to a serious incident the preceding Saturday. We were not assigned to Five West this time, but to the sixth floor of the Tower. This was the same part of the hospital where I had spent two weeks with August in December 2001 as the physicians struggled to diagnose his Stevens-Johnson syndrome. Once again, I was sitting beside August's hospital bed. This time, though, I was trying to put it all together. Ever since he had begun arching in late November 2010, I had been wondering why Dr. Sandemelir had promoted the pump so vigorously over the safer and equally effective low-tech alternative. I suddenly had two intertwining insights. First, from Dr. Sandemelir's perspective—that of a young academic physician—low-tech Botox injections were humdrum. The Relaxanoid pump, by contrast, was high-tech and prestigious. Dr. Joyce had built a considerable publishing record around it. Like any young academic, she needed to publish in order to earn promotion. Second, I saw that those behind the relatively new pump program had needed to get its numbers up. The program had to have patients to grow. Like any medical organization trying to establish itself, it was pressed to maintain cash flow and institutional support. That's why it had taken August into the program despite the fact that his being nonverbal made him a bad candidate.

This epiphany allowed me to form a coherent picture. For Ilene and me, the pump had been a horror story, an episode worthy of the TV series *Black Mirror*, one for which there was no fast-forward button. We had to live through every second of it without any respite. Ever since the implantation of the first pump in 2010, August's bedroom had become the scene of crisis after crisis. Excitement, panic, and adrenaline rush had occurred at the worst part of each turn of the cycle. And the wheel just wouldn't stop turning. Our world would become anxiety-laden and frantic as we struggled to deactivate the bomb that had been planted inside of our son.

Disenchanted, I now wanted the second pump out. I became a man with a mission, convinced that it was going to kill August. That morning I spoke to the floor's attending physician and anyone else who would listen. I asked, requested, commanded, ordered, implored, entreated, beseeched, and then begged that it be removed. I was a man running around with his hair on fire. I'm surprised now that no one called security. The attending physician tried to settle me down. He cautioned me that, given his state at the time, August couldn't be operated on anyway.

In the middle of that Monday afternoon, Dr. Sandemelir came from her clinic, again blowing through the door like a bitter wind, eager to reconvert an apostate. Again she was alone—no sign of the Yellow Man, the Hippocrates company rep. It was obvious by this point that, despite his commitment to accompany us "on each step of the journey," he had bailed.

Ever since November 2010, Dr. Sandemelir had dismissed the Full Pterodactyl as a problem that she didn't cause, so it wasn't hers to solve. On this particular Monday, once again she and I found ourselves facing one another over this same issue, she and I on opposite sides of August's bed.

"He's going to take this pump with him to the grave," I predicted.

"Pardon me?" she said, eyebrows raised and staring at me.

"The pump has to come out."

"Removing the pump will do nothing to resolve the arching," she said calmly.

"No, I want it to come out. He's going to take this pump with him to the grave!" I repeated.

She looked at me hard, baffled that I was being uncooperative. For about twenty seconds we remained silent. "Removing the pump won't change anything," she finally said.

"He's going to take this pump with him to the grave," I said a third time.

"Why do you keep saying that? Removing the pump won't solve the problem."

"Why?"

"Because," and then she leaned over the bed railing and waved her hand over August's distorted form, announcing, "this is *dystonia*."

I will never know why she waited until that moment to drop this bomb. Dystonia itself meant nothing to me; the issue was that—at this critical juncture—she suddenly and opportunistically had an answer to what August's problem was. Whatever her reason for saying this word now, I was confounded, and the sensation came like feeling a first shudder of the San Andreas. *Dystonia* was a new word.

Dystonia. It sounded like *dystopia*. The two could form a rhyme in a poem.

Why had *dystonia*—whatever it was—never been mentioned to me before? August had been suffering from the Full Pterodactyl off and on for nearly three years. In summer of 2012, he had spent sixty-four days in Bensalem-Salomon, twisted up into a jumble. More than two dozen physicians had trooped through his hospital room and viewed his arching. Not one of them though had pronounced the word *dystonia*.

"What is happening?" I said.

She looked at me blankly. "What?"

"Why did you wait until now to tell me this?"

"What do you mean?"

"Dystonia," I said. "You waited."

"Waited?"

"How long have you known? You waited until I wanted the pump to be removed to tell me that his condition was dystonia."

"No."

"Hell, yes. I see it now. If I hadn't forced your hand, you would've never said anything."

"I don't know what you mean."

"How long have you not said anything?"

"I don't know what you're talking about."

"How long have you been hiding this ace up your sleeve?"

"What are you saying?"

"How long were you planning to keep this concealed?"

"We haven't concealed anything."

"How long have you known?"

"I don't know what you are thinking, but you're wrong."

"I suppose it's just serendipity," I said. "For three years he's arching himself into a knot, and you don't know what the hell his problem is. You lead me to believe it's not your problem to solve. You say, 'Let the neurologist deal with it.' But now Ilene and I want the pump removed, and all of a sudden you know what his problem is. It's dystonia."

"It took time to diagnose."

"Three years? Give me a fucking break! You expect me to believe that? But wait! Are you just making this diagnosis up?"

Her expression indicated that this was a ridiculous thing to say. "This is dystonia," she said, trying to maintain her composure. "It's a movement disorder in the same family as Parkinson's disease."

"Yes, okay. What now?"

In a low voice she said, "There's a dystonia clinic operating at the medical school."

This information took a moment to register. And then I was thunderstruck.

"What? You're fucking kidding me, right? There's a clinic within driving distance? A clinic nearby? But no one thought to tell us about it? There was August, arching for all to see, off and on for almost three years, displaying this condition before an army of medical professionals, living a life in hell, and it didn't occur to you or anyone else to inform us that his condition was dystonia and that there's a clinic nearby?"

"No," she said, "you have it all wrong."

"No. I don't have it all wrong. What is there here to be wrong about! You haven't done the best you could do for August."

"We've done the best we can do for August."

"Like fuck you have! Do you not see what you've done? Can't you see? You've destroyed him. You've destroyed my son!"

"Calm down! Get a grip on yourself. We've done—"

"You're the one who talked me into this."

"Wait! What? No! The pump was indicated based on the patient's medical profile."

"This pump was your idea!"

"I encouraged you to consider the pump because it was the better of two options."

"The pump has been a fucking disaster! I wish we'd never met you or that scrofulous shitbag, Dr. Joyce."

"The pump has nothing to do with what is happening now."

I stared at her in disbelief. She was insulting my intelligence.

"As I've told you many times," she said, "there is no way that the pump can be implicated."

"There is no way that the pump can be implicated," I repeated in mockery. "And while I'm on it," I said, slightly changing the subject, "the one lesson you should take away from this sorry episode is this: you should never again implant a Relaxanoid pump in a nonverbal child."

I'd struck a nerve. Dr. Sandemelir stepped back, as if stung by the charge, and then said in an icily adversarial tone, "His being nonverbal has nothing to do with any of this."

"He was a bad candidate from the start," I said. "But you needed patients. And while you are at it, feed me that line again, you know, the one about 'we've come a long way!' About medicine's great strides."

"But we *have* come a long way."

"That's cold comfort," I said. "How many people died yesterday to get us to where we are today. Medicine sits on top of a graveyard."

"We're just human beings," she replied vehemently. "What do you expect? Do you think we understand everything in advance? Do you think we are perfect? Do you think we arrive on the scene all-knowing?"

"Give me a fucking break! Every one of you acts like you're all-knowing!"

"No. You give *me* a break! You and your wife came to us and said, 'Please do something.' And we are doing something with the knowledge we have. We don't set out to hurt people. We don't experiment on them. We try to help them. And, yes, people have died despite our best efforts. What we've learned from their deaths has brought us to where we are today. It's a cumulative process. It's the scientific method. It's how we advance."

"I thought the history of medicine was over!"

She looked at me surprised. "Whatever ever made you think that? It's never over."

"Then history is a nightmare," I said, dismayed beyond all reckoning. "I thought that all of the advances had already been made! I thought the pump's experimental phase was over. I had no idea you were still beta testing. I never would have agreed! I didn't sign him up for this! I don't want my son to be cannon fodder for future victories. What if it was your child? Would you sacrifice *your* child on the altar of progress?"

This got through to her. Her mood abruptly shifted, the expression on her face morphing from confrontation to apprehension. Having two young children of her own, she understood. The loss of our children—how could we ever bear that. For a moment the two of us stood silent and still, staring into the abyss.

"It was selfish of me," I continued more quietly, "but I wanted him to benefit from yesterday's victories, not contribute to tomorrow's. I didn't volunteer him to help some future kid. What are tomorrow's victories to him? Or to me? I just want my son back, the way he was before the pump."

A few minutes later Dr. Sandemelir left, and that was the last time I spoke with her. After she was gone, I called Ilene. I immediately and sheepishly admitted that I had yelled at the doctor. Then I told her that Dr. Sandemelir had diagnosed August's arching as dystonia and had informed me that a dystonia clinic was operating eighty miles away.

"Dystonia," she repeated, not as a question. "Of course." And then there was a long pause. "I should have thought of that myself. I don't know why it didn't occur to me." And then there was another silence as the implication sank in further. "It's not just dystonia, but *severe* dystonia." Then she observed, angrily, "She waited until we wanted the pump to come out to tell us this?" Another break in the conversation followed, and then she said, "So what's going to happen now?"

"Here's my idea. August is going to remain under Dr. Sandemelir's care for the time being. We'll gradually turn the pump down to taper him off Relaxanoid and avoid drug withdrawal. And then in a month or two, when he's in better shape, we'll schedule a surgery to remove the pump."

She contemplated the idea for a moment. "So your idea is we'll go back to Botox injections and oral Relaxanoid?"

"Yeah."

There were a few seconds of silence. "Okay. That sounds about right. That's a good plan."

"And once August's recovered from the surgery, I'll drive him to this dystonia clinic to see if anyone there can help him."

"Sounds like a plan. So somehow we'll get back to July 7, 2010?" she asked, hungry for encouragement.

"Yeah, we'll get back. Give or take a few hours. Don't worry, we'll be the lucky ones."

We gave each other our usual sign-off, "Love, love," and hung up.

———

That Monday evening Katrina arrived at six to watch August in his hospital room. I went for a jog. When I returned, I noticed that August was starting to develop a little runny nose. He had had many such sniffles before. Already that day, he had shown considerable improvement, and I assumed that things were on the mend. Having a lot of grading to catch up with, I prepared to go home.

August was lying in the hospital bed wearing an orange T-shirt and a diaper. Arching as he was, he was now batting away again at his noisy Activity Atom and giggling. And then I heard it, the laugh of Medusa.

Katrina said, "What's so funny, Augie?"

I felt relieved. It was a sign that he was feeling better.

At 7:45 p.m. I left him in Katrina's care. But before leaving the hospital, I made a point of speaking with his night nurse, Madison. She had just come on shift. Young, pale-skinned, fresh-faced, she was a newly minted product of the nursing program at UNF. I had spoken with her before, and I knew that she wanted to do a good job. This was her first full-time position. She had dreamed of one day becoming a nurse and working at a children's hospital. Now that day had arrived.

"Please keep a close eye on my little boy tonight."

"I certainly will, Mr. Gabbard," she said, nodding enthusiastically. "I will check in on him frequently."

I left the building under moonlight: a waxing gibbous moon had passed the zenith. When I was pulling out of the parking lot I remembered that I hadn't given August a kiss the way I usually did when leaving. *I'll give him an extra kiss tomorrow morning*, I thought as I drove away. I planned to return to the hospital a little after six the next morning, Tuesday, to get him ready to go home.

Katrina remained with August until after he had fallen asleep. That was at 10 p.m.

At a little past midnight, Ilene and I had just fallen asleep when her cell phone rang. She answered, and someone on the other end told her that August was having trouble breathing. We decided that I should go back to the hospital and that she would remain behind with Clio, who was asleep and too young to be left alone in the house.

As I approached them this time, the glass doors of the hospital did not shoot back a reflection: light emanated from within. I took the elevator. On the sixth floor of the Tower, a broad well-lit corridor appeared when the door opened and, beyond it, a set of white double doors. Someone on the other side, at the nurses' station, would have to press a buzzer to allow me in.

In the sight of him was no bode of dawn. I knew instantly that we were never going wind up the lucky ones. Madison was distraught. The floodwaters had risen too high, and no wise old sorcerer was coming to make them recede.

I called Ilene. Our neighbor across the driveway, Suzanne Honeycutt, came over to stay with Clio, who remained asleep. Ilene soon arrived, and we assembled in the same room where hours earlier I had said to Dr. Sandemelir, "He's going to take this pump with him to the grave."

The Kangaroo had been turned off. August was unconscious. The sniffles had turned into pneumonia. It had come on quickly, the way these things sometimes do with children. In his contorted posture, he hadn't been able to clear his fluids. His breathing now was exceedingly labored. This was the death rattle I had heard when Dad lay dying nineteen years earlier. I knew now why John Keats had written the line "a living death was in each gush of sounds." He had nursed his brother Tom when he was dying of tuberculosis. This was what death sounded like.

Although we could have, Ilene and I didn't request that August be placed on a ventilator. The attending physician, Dr. Choudhury, a young woman from India, didn't try to change our minds. She asked if we wanted him to be given morphine. We did. Morphine impedes respiration. August's breath came slower and slower.

"I switched to pediatrics," Dr. Choudhury said, tears welling in her eyes, "to avoid scenes like this."

It was strange to be with our son and not hear the Kangaroo, so accustomed to its sound had we become. We couldn't tell how much consciousness remained, so Ilene and I took turns whispering in his ear. When it was my turn, I sang the "Good Morning Song." You never understand the difference between life and death so clearly as when you are watching someone die. Death is a maelstrom that sucks us in. August was going in before me.

"My darling boy," I whispered in his ear, "my moon and stars."

In his ending was his beginning. At nearly the same hour of the early morning that he had been born fourteen years earlier, he died in our arms. We laid him on the bed, and Dr. Choudhury lifted his left arm from the linen and held it at the wrist. A large-faced analog clock was mounted on the wall behind her. She glanced over her shoulder to note the official time, announcing in a neutral tone, "2:20 a.m."

And that was that. Afterward, there wasn't much more to say about August except that he had been the boy who'd made one little room an everywhere.

X

THE MORNING AUGUST DIED, ILENE AND I BROKE
the news to Clio. It was still the early morning. She was
eleven, two weeks short of turning twelve. She was in her
bed, and when she understood what we'd said, she bolted up
and ran wailing through the house to his bedroom. There
she threw herself down on his empty bed and howled. And
there she remained a long time. The saddest part of someone
you love dying is knowing that he will never come back to
hear you say you love him. In the years following she took
her brother's death stoically. Too stoically, perhaps. Almost
four years afterward, when she was nearly sixteen, she was
walking in the neighborhood and saw a car's tire run over
a butterfly. She burst into tears and immediately called her
mother to tell her what had happened.

In the months following August's death, I was pierced
with regret each time I remembered something that I had
intended to do for him but had never gotten around to doing. A thousand little pangs. I walked through San Marco
Square, past the fountain and bronze lions and Starbucks,
gazing upon the luxurious shops as though they were the
storefronts of a Potemkin village. I drove in a daze by Craig
Creek and through the streets of my well-heeled suburban

neighborhood, oblivious of the stately homes with their harmonious landscaping. I saw the swanky houses on Alhambra Drive with Jaguars and Jeeps and Land Rovers parked in their driveways and with their fussy front yards, an exhibition of the prosperous arrogance of a world in which death had no place. But now I knew that dwelling behind these façades was the inevitability of death. Death no longer was an abstraction. For me it had become the only truth.

Some of our friends mistakenly assumed that August's death brought great relief for Ilene and me. It is true that attending to a boy who couldn't do anything for himself had made the days hectic. Such caregiving required round-the-clock attention and meticulous tending and planning. But, despite the difficulty, every day Ilene and I had sallied forth with a sense of purpose. We never questioned what was important because we knew. Over time, the caregiving, a deceptively rewarding practice, had become deeply entrenched in our psyches and allowed bonds more intimate and intense to develop than those between most parents and their typically developing children. To care for a child dependent in every way, day after day for many years, is to build up an emotional communion beyond the average person's comprehension. In every possible activity, we had to serve as our son's eyes, hands, and feet. Caregiving was taxing, time-consuming, and exhausting; a laborious, never-ending responsibility; an undertaking that was emotionally, physically, and financially draining. Yet it was also a tremendous event, a peak experience, the defining time of our lives. And now we grieved for its loss as well as for the loss of our child.

The death of a son or daughter is the second club you never ask to join. *My little child*, Ilene would think, *you never did come home.* August was a poem in a collection that had gone back to the library. His possessions remained untouched in the little elfin grot at the back of the house, the small room with a white door, the walls of windmill wings blue, and his electric hospital bed in its southwest corner. In the first months after his death I used to curl up in that bed and lie there among his sheets and pillows and abandoned toys, his ghostly hand stroking my hair. I felt as though the spirit of the world had died. The days of being an ironic dad were over. There was no way to be ironic about this. Irony was broken. I had found in life the one thing that was true, and now he was gone. The best joke I could muster was that, like many good men before him, August died in the Tower. But there was nothing ironic about this statement, and the most I could manage to accompany it was a grim smile.

When I wasn't overcome with grief, I was filled with vengeful fury. I wasn't as unsettled as the people you sometimes see on an urban street, muttering, gesturing, rehashing past wrongs, but these visibly disturbed people suddenly made sense to me. All of the angry people in the world now made sense. They made sense because I had become one of them. Every time I drove by Bensalem-Salomon, I wanted to burn it to the ground. I wanted to burn down the house of medicine. Our story was sad and tragic, but it wasn't unique. Credible sources estimate that tens of thousands of Americans, if not hundreds of thousands, die every year from medical mistakes. Medical error is reportedly the third leading cause of death in the United States. So there was good reason to be angry. Songs from the band Linkin Park filled my iTunes playlist for listening when I went running. In one, the late Chester Bennington belts out the lyrics to

"Burn It Down." Hearing it, my heart would pump a little harder. I would run a little faster.

Ilene and I eventually decided that the moment had arrived to sort through August's things. We would donate some of them to charity, keep others, and discard the rest. We sold the electric hospital bed. The family continued to call this *August's room* even though I had moved into it, transferring my home office from the front of the house: the computer, desk, bookcase, and a filing cabinet. The bookcase was placed in the corner of the room where the electric bed had been. I didn't paint the walls or baseboards or door when I moved in, so I was surrounded by windmill-wings blue.

When I sat at my computer, the room's east-facing window was behind my left shoulder. Out that way I could see the neighbors' grassy yard filled with gigantic oaks. Clumps of Spanish moss hung from the foliage like ghosts a recent hurricane had flung into them. Through gaps in the moss and branches appeared broken bits of sky. Beneath them were shrapnel-gray shards of the Duck Pond. As before, at a certain time of the morning during a certain time of the year before spring, a ray of sunlight would shoot through this window and land on the wall to my right. It would be the color of Laughing Orange.

Nineteen months after August's death, in June 2015, I pulled out the birth records. The document stack was seven inches high. Following the dismissal of the lawsuit in 2004, Buchanan & Buchanan had shipped this material to us via UPS. For nearly eleven years the box containing these papers had been gathering dust in a closet. On a rainy afternoon,

I carried the stack to my desk and started going through it. It was completely disorganized. With August's passing I now had the time to read carefully through the documents. At last I had a chance to solve what I'd been calling "the mystery of the ear," the reason for the ear-shaped abrasion on August's forehead at birth. Sixteen years earlier, the four doctors at the family consult at Loma Prieta had gaslighted us, not wanting to say anything that might lead to a lawsuit. What was it that they wouldn't tell us?

I took solace in going back and reading about August's beginning. Sifting through the sheets offered a means of holding on to his memory. They brought back events that I had forgotten. The prince of indeterminacy was gone, but this material made me feel close to him. Arranging the papers chronologically seemed to be the first thing to do. A lot of pages had to be sorted through, and many were duplicates. Slowly they gained a semblance of order.

Ilene didn't want to look at them. She found the idea too painful. Of the two of us, one had given birth, the other had only witnessed. As with her mother's death when she was nine, she viewed August's birth as the worst of traumas. It was a laceration in time, and no healing could ever occur.

Not that I blamed her for not wanting to look at the birth records. Examining them would only raise troubling and unanswerable questions about what we should have done or done differently.

"Why are you doing this?" she asked me one afternoon.

"I want to know what happened to our son," I replied.

"But why?" said Ilene. "What's the point? It won't change anything."

Ilene stood in the white-framed doorway. I was sitting at my desk but had turned my chair around to face her. In the days immediately following August's death a year and a half earlier, she and I had found ourselves screaming at each other. We didn't know why. The reasons reached beyond fathom. Our outbursts exceeded blaming each other. They came from a pain so deep we thought it had no bottom. We were wounded animals with no place to lie down. Ilene began seeing a therapist, and I started writing this book.

Screaming at each other turned out to be a brief phase, and we began to speak lovingly again. Anne Bradstreet wrote, "If ever two were one, then surely we"—a sentiment that is true for us. And we got a dog, and he became our comfort animal. And almost every morning we started getting up early to run together, something we had not been able to do when August was alive. If it was still dark outside, she wore a flashing blue light on her back and I, a red one. From the rear, we resembled a distant police car with its lights flashing.

"You want justice, don't you," she said that afternoon, walking over and standing in front of where I was seated. There was no hint of criticism in her voice, but the statement also wasn't framed as a question. It was more of a comment, an observation, a realization, as though the thought had just struck her at that very moment that this was what I was up to.

"The law let us down."

"Yes, it did."

"I want justice for August," I admitted. "It's my duty as his father."

"Well, there isn't any justice," she said in a neutral tone tinged with resignation. "And there won't be any either. At least not for August. The world isn't like that."

"Then what is the world like? What is there any of?"

She was silent. Had I stumped her? But no. Placing her hand on my shoulder, she said, "There is only love."

For months I went about the task of studying the birth files by fits and starts. But I was a slacker: I would come back to the documents after letting them sit untouched for weeks. Searching for an answer was like looking for a line at the bottom of the sea. I began to wonder if perhaps Ilene and I had been wrong to focus all of our attention on the test results of February 22 and March 1. On these two dates the personnel of the OB-GYN practice had conducted stress tests on the fetus, and the results had been poor.

We had assumed that the practice had not responded diligently to these indicators of a potentially bad outcome and so had been negligent. The baby was already in trouble, we had thought, when we arrived early Wednesday morning, March 3, at the hospital for induction and delivery. But now I started examining instead the labor process itself, the events taking place between the morning of March 3 and that of March 5.

Was something that happened in the delivery suite during that time the cause of August's problems? Dr. Latchesik had stated under oath in her deposition that it wasn't until 3:33 a.m. on the morning of March 5 that she first learned that a serious problem had developed. She said that at 3:33 a.m. the problem had, in her words, "already begun."

I went meticulously through the birth records, looking for a mention of the per diem nurse, who had been our main labor and delivery nurse, but I did not find one. So I called Joanne. She was Joanne Bluhen now and living on Alameda

Island with husband Kevin and four children. We had last seen her when she and other friends joined us to disperse most of August's ashes into the waves at Tennessee Valley Beach in Marin County.

"Cowboy!" she said, recognizing my voice, "a blast from the past!" Then she added in her faux Southern accent, "What's shakin'?" After a moment's pause, she added, softly, "Natsukashii," a term she then told me that her mother used. She explained that it was a word for remembering, a feeling of nostalgia, a fondness when experiencing something for the first time in a long time.

We chatted for a while, and then I got around to the reason why I'd called, to get information about the morning of August's birth. She said she couldn't remember much about it, at least nothing specific.

"What did you tell our lawyer when he deposed you?"

"Deposed me? No one ever deposed me."

"What? No one ever deposed you?" I was shocked. "You never talked to our attorney, Byron Greyscale?"

"No. No one ever contacted me."

"That's strange. What about the hospital attorney?"

"No, never heard from him either."

"Hmmm. Do you remember, in the hour before the birth, the two nurses and the resident talking about the baby's heart rate?"

"Oh, man! Do you expect me to remember that?"

"The black nurse in her thirties, you know, and the very young white nurse? The black nurse was the main labor and delivery nurse. They talked about the heart rate? And the resident, she came over and said that the heart rate must be Mom's?"

She paused for a long while and then said, "No, I don't recall anything about that. But, then, I was gone for a while. Remember? I'd gone back to my apartment and then returned. The birth suite was deserted, and then everyone came back, and then the birth happened. So, I can't help you about that."

I had no choice but to peer through a glass darkly on my own. And yet, as Lucy Grealy observes, "Sometimes it is as difficult to know what the past holds as it is to know the future."

It was March 5, 1999. The clock on the wall behind the blond woman at the nurses' station read 3:23 a.m. "Everyone's giving birth," she told me, then added that the doctors were "very busy." I said, "I just want them to know that my wife is ready." To this she replied, "They'll come when they can. They'll get that baby out in no time."

When I returned to the birth suite after my feckless attempt to summon a physician, I related to Ilene and Joanne what had just happened at the nurses' station. "Something of an interesting conversation, to say the least. The nurse asked me the meaning of *ready*. And then she said all the doctors are busy. No one's available. Evidently everybody's giving birth."

"You lie!" Joanne exclaimed, looking both panicked and angry.

"The nurse seemed to think this is going to be a very easy birth," I said.

"I'm going down to the nurses' station myself and make a big stink," said Joanne, and she was just about to stomp down there and complain loudly when the per diem nurse, the blond nurse, and the third nurse returned all at once.

"Are you guys back with us?" asked Joanne in a hostile tone.

"We're here," said the per diem nurse.

Dr. Atropski, the resident physician, soon followed them in. By now it was 3:28 a.m., and the four of them then didn't do anything. They seemed to be waiting for something.

Finally, at 3:33 a.m., Dr. Latchesik, the attending physician, came into the suite and immediately gowned and gloved up. The last time Ilene, Joanne, and I had seen her was at 3:03 a.m., at which time the resident had told her that a problem was occurring with the electronic fetal monitor. Now, at 3:33, as she prepared herself for delivering the baby, Dr. Latchesik asked, "There was a problem with the monitor?" A short and seemingly casual discussion followed about whose heart rate the now-detached fetal monitor had been reading at 2:55 a.m. Given the low numbers, Dr. Latchesik quickly affirmed with a characteristically decisive little head bob whose heartbeat it must have been. "Yes, it must have been the mother's," she said. The two doctors were completely at ease, exhibiting no sense of urgency.

Suddenly a specially dispatched pediatric team of seven or eight residents and medical students roared through the door with the self-importance of a college football squad taking the field. Why they were there or who summoned them I had no idea. This was at about 3:35 a.m. They wheeled with them a small table and used it to establish a makeshift station ten feet to the left of Ilene's bed.

The residents and medical students were full of good cheer, acting as if the baby had already been born. The only female among them was a tall, young, and slender woman with a long black ponytail, Dr. Wang, a senior resident physician. She was more serious in bearing than the other team members. Later that day she came to speak with us, to express her concern. She was the only one of all the medical professionals present in the delivery suite that morning who did.

The baby's head began to crown. Was this at 3:41? Joanne and I were positioned on opposite sides of the bed. I was holding Ilene's left hand, Joanne her right. Ilene seemed stupefied but determined to finish the process. Dr. Latchesik went down on one knee between her legs and told Joanne and me to say "Push!" in unison every few seconds.

It must have been at 3:42 that I saw Dr. Latchesik's eyes pop wide open. Her attention became tightly focused, like those of a pilot when a plane suddenly shows signs of trouble in flight. She called to the nearby team, "There's an abrasion on the baby's head!" Then she shouted, "We're going to use the vacuum!" Dr. Atropski and the per diem nurse sprang into action and swiftly readied the gear. Standing again, Latchesik positioned the vacuum-extraction device and told Ilene to push, and Ilene obeyed, and then came another order to push, and on the third try there was a great whoosh, liquid gushing, and with a flood of brownish amniotic fluid, the infant tumbled out headfirst.

The body that emerged at 3:44 a.m. was gray, limp, and lifeless. The umbilical cord was wrapped twice around his neck. Dr. Latchesik hurriedly clamped and cut the cord and handed the newborn to Dr. Atropski behind her, who whisked him over to the specially dispatched team where Dr. Wang and the residents were waiting. The team began attempting to resuscitate him.

Everyone's activity seemed frantic, and everyone whose faces we could see had wide-open eyes and grim "Oh no!"

expressions. All the while, the baby didn't cry. He didn't make any sound at all. For the first minute, most of what Ilene, Joanne, and I could see was the scrum of residents' and students' backs.

Dr. Latchesik was the first to regain her composure. She was standing near Ilene's delivery bed, and she informed us, reassuringly, "The baby is merely stunned." Contradicting this verbal assertion, though, were the apprehensive looks of others, whose faces were becoming more and more visible. Some of them had begun glancing back at us, to check our reaction. Dr. Wang and I exchanged glances, and I knew then that things were going very badly.

I wasn't looking at Joanne, but I heard her mumble, "I can't believe this is happening."

The per diem nurse walked toward Ilene's bed, moving so slowly that she seemed to advance frame by frame, as if all of this was the footage of a dream. As she approached, she held my gaze as though communicating something important. Like everyone else's (except for Dr. Latchesik's), her eyes were wide open and worried.

Dr. Latchesik spoke again, as calmly as before: "This sort of thing happens all the time." We were all waiting for the baby to breathe. But how many minutes were going by? When he finally began breathing, everyone exhaled. It was cause for celebration. Still, the newborn wasn't crying or making a sound loud enough to hear. I could tell from her demeanor that Dr. Wang was convinced that a calamity was still unfolding. Not so the others. A little party had broken out: the residents were cheering and the students started high-fiving. Dr. Wang quickly shushed them.

"Show Mom and Dad the baby!" called Dr. Latchesik optimistically. She was still standing beside Ilene's bed. A male resident next to Dr. Wang complied, and he hoisted the little body high into the air, a trophy of medical rescue.

As I went through August's birth-related papers in 2015, I returned to one of our attorney Byron Greyscale's last letters, the one dated June 28, 2004. As I was rereading, a sentence jumped out in a way that it hadn't before: "With all of the evidence establishing that August was delivered within 10 minutes of the bradycardia, we cannot establish that [the hospital] was negligent in its care and treatment of you and August."

Dr. Latchesik had claimed in her deposition that the thirty-minute bradycardia clock began ticking at around 3:33 a.m. But did more than one clock exist? Another might have started at 2:55 a.m.

Earlier in the same letter, Byron had written, "Dr. Baelish re-reviewed the heart rate tracing and believes that the heart rate seen on the heart monitor tracing is Ilene's and not August's."

At 2:55 a.m. Dr. Atropski had said that the sluggish heartbeat—80 beats per minute when it should have been 110 to 160—"must be Mom's." The per diem nurse had voiced doubt about this, suspecting that the heartbeat was the baby's.

I remembered that shortly after August's birth, a friend of Ilene's, Dr. Romano, a pediatric neurologist, had said that the electronic fetal monitor (EFM) was unreliable. And in August's case no one had relied on a monitor. I went online to read up on EFM and found the guidelines of the American Congress of Obstetricians and Gynecologists, which state, "When EFM is used during labor, the nurse or physicians should review it frequently." I also found a May 1999 article in *American Family Physician* examining the limits of EFM, which evidently are numerous. It reported that some clinicians believe that EFM provides valuable information but that it takes an expert to properly interpret the results. Had Dr. Atropski not been enough of an expert? About EFM I started repeating something in my head: *It was unreliable, and no one relied on it.* But this mantra didn't have an itinerary. I didn't know where to go with it.

I began wondering about Dr. Latchesik and her knowledge of a problem with the monitor.

And I had another thought. Even if the monitor was unreliable and everyone had assumed that the fetal heart rate given by the monitor was the mother's, didn't this then mean that the baby's heartbeat was going unmonitored? The fact that he was not being monitored did not rule out that he was experiencing distress. Equally possible, might the reading have indicated that the baby's heartbeat had become too weak to detect and so was being overridden by the mother's? Wouldn't this too have indicated distress? And I had yet another thought: surely the medical experts involved had already thought about these things.

Whether the monitor was reliable or unreliable, the per diem nurse had detected a problem. Being an outsider, perhaps she wasn't used to the way things were done at Loma Prieta, so she had noticed something that the others didn't and pointed it out, but no one listened. Did they ignore her because she was the only black person working on an all-white crew? Was it because she was a per diem? Did these factors combine to render her invisible? Did I contribute to her invisibility? After all, I myself never bothered to catch her name. In his memoir *Black Man in a White Coat*,

Dr. Damon Tweedy notes that the input of African American medical professionals is often discounted. Had the others in August's delivery suite listened to what the black nurse had to say, our son's outcome probably would have been immensely better. I have no doubt that he would be alive today.

It now seemed obvious that Dr. Latchesik mistook the time in her deposition. She claimed that she had learned of bradycardia at 3:33 a.m., but she didn't become aware of it until 3:42. I had seen her eyes pop wide open—that's how I knew. Yet, regarding the legal case, I'm not sure what difference fudging the time would have made. In another vein, I could see that, in the early morning of March 5, the sheer number of births occurring at once had overwhelmed the staff. I also now understood that skepticism about EFM had become prevailing wisdom. Dr. Atropski and Dr. Latchesik had a shared disregard for it, and this was a mistake, but I could understand why they made it. They were doing what made sense to them.

What I couldn't understand, however, was why Dr. Baelish had been so quick to gloss over the error occurring at 2:55 a.m. He had reviewed the fetal heart tracings for that time and, with the benefit of twenty-twenty hindsight, should have been able to see that the resident's misjudgment had swelled into a self-echoing, self-certifying chorus. I could only assume that he had given Dr. Latchesik's deposition testimony extraordinary weight. But why? Why would he do this?

I lay in bed, mulling over all of this, and then I got up and padded as quietly as I could through our house with groaning floorboards to August's room at the back, now my man cave. It must have been maybe 4:30 or 5 a.m. I opened the door and turned on the computer. In the little elfin grot, both windows were dark. Through the east-facing window I could see the black silhouette of the foliage in the neighbors' yard against a slightly less dark slate sky. I Googled *Dr. Lisette Atropski.* She was now working in San Diego. Next, I Googled *Dr. Sandra Latchesik.* As I learned about her, a picture began to form, and I switched from Google to my university's databases. After a bit more searching, there it was, as conspicuous as a bright-orange trail marker. She was a leader in the field of obstetrics and gynecology, having published a large number of articles. At the end of 1999, a few months after August's birth, she had been appointed to head an OB-GYN department at a top teaching hospital in Chicago.

Then, in 2010, La Brea Medical Center (a pseudonym), another of the nation's top teaching hospitals, recruited her to become the chair of its Department of Obstetrics and Gynecology. According to that hospital's magazine, she was "a nationally renowned expert" in maternal-fetal medicine and a prolific author of peer-reviewed publications.

It was 5:50 a.m. In the eastern sky appeared crepuscular light presaging a gray morning. Was it possible that Dr. Baelish had deferred to an eminent authority? I Googled *Dr. James Baelish.* Three people with that name were practicing medicine in the United States, but only one was an OB-GYN. Since the late 2000s, this one had been practicing in Springfield, Missouri. Was this him? This doctor had been working at UCLA in the early 2000s, so, yes, this had to be him.

Leaving Google and returning to the databases, I found that Baelish too was an accomplished scholar, although he was not nearly the high flier that Latchesik was. He had published thirty-two articles, all of them in a single academic medical journal. I wanted to learn more about Baelish, so for the next forty minutes I tried different keyword combinations on Google. I was like someone at the slots in a casino, trying to hit a jackpot.

And then I found something. *Slate* had recently reprinted an article from the mid-1990s in which Dr. Baelish was mentioned. What especially caught my eye was information about where he was working in 1996: he was "the director of the high-risk obstetric unit" at La Brea Medical Center.

The identification of Baelish with La Brea raised a question. Were the positions at this medical school and hospital that Latchesik and Baelish held the same or closely aligned? Moreover, both doctors were perinatologists, and this made me wonder: in California, how big could that field be?

More searching in the databases revealed that in 2007 Latchesik was appointed to the editorial board of the obstetrics and gynecology journal that had published all thirty-two of Dr. Baelish's articles. She joined the board long after he had published there.

What was I to make of these findings? There was nothing inherently incriminating about the two doctors being leaders in the same subspecialty and having ties to the same journal and to the same hospital and medical school. These discoveries seemed to be more than mere coincidences but less than smoking guns.

At best, these discoveries were meaningful indicators. Neither doctor was laboring in obscurity. Both were well-known physicians in their field. Both were perinatologists. Dr. Baelish was a respected elder figure, and Dr. Latchesik was a startlingly bright up-and-comer. In all likelihood, Baelish would have spotted Latchesik's rising star. At the very least, he would have served as a peer reviewer on at least one of her many journal articles, and it is likely that they would have crossed paths at conferences. The chance that the two didn't know each other was next to nil. In the birth records that Byron had sent him, the names had not been redacted. Dr. Baelish would have seen that the defendant was Dr. Latchesik. He would have recognized the name.

Now I knew what the question was that Ilene and I should have asked back in June 2004, in our last communication with Byron. We should have inquired whether someone had tracked down the per diem nurse in Sacramento. Byron was right: her name appeared nowhere in the birth records. I surmised that no one had gone to the trouble of questioning her. The per diem had disappeared from the documents and notes, if her name had ever been in them. Without her, the legal case could never have gone forward. If my memory was correct, and if the per diem nurse had been deposed, she would have challenged Dr. Latchesik's claim that bradycardia didn't start until 3:33 a.m. She would have said that it started at 2:55 a.m.

But there was something that rendered the per diem's testimony irrelevant. Byron had written, "Dr. Baelish re-reviewed the heart rate tracing, and believes that the heart rate seen on the heart monitor tracing is Ilene's and not August's." Why was he so aggressively shooting down the possibility that the heartbeat might have been August's? To be cleared of malpractice, Dr. Latchesik needed the heartbeat at 2:55 to be the mother's. Was that why?

Dr. Baelish's assertion that the heartbeat was the mother's ran contrary to what took place forty-nine minutes later. The only empirical way to assess the accuracy of this "expert opinion" would have been to weigh it against the outcome. However, a healthy birth did not take place. The outcome at 3:44 a.m. did not logically match Baelish's assertion about what was happening at 2:55 a.m. The one did not follow from the other. In fact, the two together formed a non sequitur.

And that's when the reality hit me. We should never have fired the pit bull attorney Allan Lerch. Byron didn't notice the non sequitur. Or, more likely, he didn't spend enough time thinking about it. The most charitable construction one could put upon Dr. Baelish's reading of the data was that it was exceedingly conservative. The feminist literary scholar Sandra Gilbert, who successfully litigated her husband's wrongful death at the UC Davis Medical Center, relates a remarkably similar situation in her 1997 book *Wrongful Death*. In it she reports her attorney telling her, "Our guy [the outside medical expert that the attorney himself had hired] . . . is being very conservative. . . . Haven't I told you all along? These guys don't like to testify against each other, they're very *very* careful about what they say, what they're *willing* to say." Byron, though, didn't have the courtesy to tell us that much, if he even thought of it. He made no effort whatsoever to contextualize Baelish's reading of the evidence. He just accepted it at face value. And once Baelish had thrown cold water on August's case, thus making a settlement seem less likely, Byron unceremoniously dumped us. No point remained in deposing the per diem nurse in Sacramento. Even if she verified that Dr. Atropski had discussed a low heart rate at 2:55 a.m. with the nurses, Baelish had already rendered the issue moot.

I learned two lessons from this sixteen-year odyssey that started in 1999. I found out that it is a lot harder to sue for medical malpractice than people think. And I discovered that, while science may serve humankind, humans can corrupt science.

One day Ilene came home from her physical therapy practice, the one she had come to own, and told me that she had had an interesting conversation with one of her patients, Dr. Hermes. An anesthesiologist in his early sixties, he was a physician who often served on obstetric cases at a local hospital.

During the session the conversation turned to August's birth, and, at his behest, she told him the story. When she finished, he remained silent for a moment, and then he said, "I can't say for certain what happened. But this sounds like a classic case of an obstructed labor." He went on to explain: "This is also known as labor dystocia, and it occurs because the baby can't exit the pelvis during childbirth due to being blocked. This happens even if the uterus is contracting normally."

"I had a lot of pain in my pelvic area despite the epidural," Ilene said.

"His head might have been hitting against the pelvic bone," Dr. Hermes went on. "It'd be like ramming your head into a door, slowly but repeatedly. Like this," he said, and he slammed his fist into his palm, then paused, then slammed it again, and again paused. *Bam!* Pause. *Bam!* Pause. *Bam!* Pause. *Bam!*

Stories of medical errors are easy to dismiss, but a close family member of his had recently experienced a serious one, so he was open to the idea. And then he said something that was unprecedented, for us at least: "Someone should have noticed," he told Ilene, "that the labor wasn't progressing and ordered a C-section. I am truly sorry that August received such poor care. That shouldn't have happened."

"Then a medical error isn't just a figment of our imaginations?"

He chuckled quietly, shook his head, and said, "Is *that* what they wanted you to believe? Listen, here's what probably happened. It's not complicated. August experienced fetal distress during the delivery, and maybe he was experiencing it in the days leading up to the delivery. But whenever it started, it wasn't detected, and as a result he suffered severe brain injury and cerebral palsy. And that's why he had the life he did."

The answer to a riddle seems so obvious once it is revealed. After Ilene came home and related Dr. Hermes's opinion on the matter, three words formed a permanent rhyme in my mind. The rhyme summed up the story of August's life:

dys-toc-i-a,

dys-ton-i-a,

dys-top-i-a.

AFTERWORD

I AM IN AUGUST'S OLD ROOM, NOW MY MAN CAVE.
It is 6:40 a.m. on Thursday, March 5, and it is sixty degrees
Fahrenheit outside. It is a gloriously tranquil time in our
backyard garden, which appears through one of this room's
two windows, the south-facing one. Peering through it I
have a close-to-the-earth perspective. The garden is lit by
the pale light of predawn. To see it, I have to peer around the
large desktop computer monitor. In May 2014, four young
and energetic landscapers arrived one morning to install this
memorial garden, a bereavement gift, which I call Parvaneh,
from the Persian word for *butterfly*. A landscape architect
designed it. The four men scraped away what remained of
a scraggily lawn and populated the space with porterweed,
milkweed, penta, and trailing rosemary. In the center they
placed a dwarf Persian lime tree. Then they laid down a
thick bed of pine-straw mulch a richer and redder brown
than the sandy soil beneath.

Already in place in this backyard were three trees—an
oak, a maple, and a birch. During the late morning and
early afternoon hours they provide shade, but through their
spotty foliage enough light glimmers to keep this nursery happy. The landscape architect selected plants likely

to attract butterflies, and, as intended, the Monarchs have found their way. In the midst of the lush foliage their wings quiver. From time to time they alight on the dwarf Persian lime, the heart of the bower. On a typical day at noon, its little green leaves and balls of fruit glint in the intense light. Mixed among the tree's roots are some of August's ashes.

This morning I awakened prematurely from a dream in which I vividly saw him. In it he was laughing, the laugh of Medusa. A line from Our Song, "Losing My Religion," comes back: "I thought that I heard you laughing, but that was just a dream." With the dawn's first glow I had climbed out of bed—quietly so as not to awaken Ilene—and padded through the house to the little elfin grot, where I sat at my desk and uttered my aubade: "Wakee, wakee." But I understood all too well that he never would. Outside, the predawn radiance unveiled the bird-filled world, and through the east-facing window the neighbors' oaks silhouetted the lilac sky. After another ten minutes or so I heard Clio, the coffee muse, grinding beans.

Clio has big brown eyes, and these days she wears a T-shirt that says "Merde." She has her own mind. Yesterday she said to me, "I'm going to be a better person than you." When she was fifteen, I texted her saying that I was looking for a song on iTunes by Michael Kiwanuka called "Love and Hate" but couldn't find it. She replied that I was being old-fashioned. "No one buys music on iTunes anymore." She is a ballet dancer. Ballet mingles the exquisite with the excruciating, beauty with pain. The *attitude derrière* and the other contortions of her dance express a willed and graceful dystonia. It is as if she were taking August's grotesque posture and transfiguring it into art.

Today is August's birthday, and I feel a little sadder than usual. Sometimes the past catches up with me. I fall through a trap door into the events of long ago when August was alive, and these moments are painful. I can barely breathe, and I tear up. I don't have a precise word for describing this feeling more stabbing than nostalgia.

The birth records long ago fizzled into a remainder, a left-over assortment of stale facts that didn't make any difference because they couldn't give us our son back. Emily Dickinson writes, "But are not all facts dreams as soon as we put them behind us?" Where is the empirical truth now? Where has the scientific evidence gone? Men supposedly want to fix things, but what was I supposed to fix? My son was broken far beyond my power to repair. In no way could I go back in time, make things right, and save our boy. Life on earth had continued to run its course. For a time it carried August in its flow, but then one day it started to run on without him.

Solving the mystery—of what happened at his birth—has become irrelevant. Who cares now who made what mistake? I started out in anger, wanting to burn down the house of medicine, but I have arrived at an unexpected place. To everything there is a season, and that means it is time to forgive, as I myself would want to be forgiven. Who among us doesn't go into the courtroom of life demanding justice, only to find himself humbled and pleading for mercy?

What do Ilene and I have now? Throughout our house we have scuff marks and indentations on walls and door-frames. Some are deep dents. Each of these is approximately ten inches above the floor. They are the vestiges of where, as we rolled August through the house, his wheelchair's foot pedals banged. And we have August's sonogram. It resembles an old-time Polaroid snapshot. In the center, a fuzzy black-and-white image appears, a westward-moving hurricane just formed off the coast of Africa. And we have Clio and the illumination she brings. She is a wild orange lily in an Appalachian meadow.

And by far the strangest surprise of the entire adventure, I can no longer accurately call myself an atheist. I don't know what I am exactly. I have moved a long way away from the purely rationalist, materialist, and secular worldview I once held. But into what have I turned? Because of August, I became the least likely of pilgrims. I am still uncomfortable with the word *grace*, but August changed everything. For a moment, the doors of perception were cleansed.

If I could see God in August, I should be able to see God in others, even in his doctors. God is something that we humans can bring into the world. God exists in the relations between all of us. Whenever asked these days, I tick the box for *agnostic*—I have become comfortable with merely asking questions. While not categorizing myself as a believer, I do accept that the spirit dwells within me and in everyone I meet.

I was fortunate to have fallen in love with August. I was extraordinarily lucky that lightning struck. I didn't feel, or ever feel for long, that taking care of him was pointless. Loving him wasn't automatic, and it doesn't necessarily happen for other parents of significantly impaired children. If parents want to avoid going through what Ilene and I experienced, the slowly unfolding logic of the Enlightenment has already made it possible for them to do so. The rational solutions of the brave new world can spare parents from having to care for a child such as August.

Knowing what I know now, I would not avail myself of these solutions, not for all the world. There were a few times,

as I described, that I experienced the sensation while looking into August's eyes that I was staring into the face of
God. The spirit was within him, and my glimpsing it there
served as premonition of recognizing it in myself. At the
time of his birth I didn't know that he would develop into a
beguiling little fellow, that he would elicit great love from us
and from many other people, or that like a Yaqui shaman he
would introduce me to a separate reality. And I didn't know
that this separate reality was actually the world of my own
heart, my capacity to give and receive love.

Coffee fumes waft in through the crack at the bottom
of the closed door. Today there's a cerulean sky. Out the
room's south window the top branches of the tall, skinny
pine tree in the Jones's backyard catch flame in the sun's
opening beams. Within moments the treetops of the entire
neighborhood alight with fire. Laughing Orange explodes
everywhere. How grateful I am for this light! At last the
long solar eclipse is over. The sun shoots a brief horizontal
ray through the room's east window. The analog clock on my
desk says that it is 6:55 a.m. On the wall to my right lands
a golden patch of sunlight, a drop of illumination about the
size of a quarter. Windmill-wings blue surrounds this spot
of Laughing Orange—the laugh of Medusa. But I still find
myself in a quandary: in which of the two colors does the
truth lie?

Through the south window I survey Parvaneh. Let us
cultivate our garden. But oh, what birds are these? Robins? But why should I ask. They have been here all along. I
look out the other window. In the east, the sky gleams like
the burnished gold leaf of a medieval panel painting. Au-
rora. Hail, holy light, the eternal, coeternal beam! Through
the filigree of oaks and moss shines a new blazing world.

Looking into the heart of light, the silence—my eyes need a moment to adjust. August's story is a circular book, one whose ending folds back around to the first page, where I begin it over again. The end is where I start. He and I travel together. We're a couple of rich men now. Despite knowing each mile of this journey, I embrace it. *Incipit vita nova.*

ACKNOWLEDGMENTS

I WOULD LIKE TO EXPRESS MY GRATITUDE TO THE many people who helped me write this book. Among them are the brave souls who soldiered through early manuscript versions and gave me emotional support and constructive feedback. This list includes Rachel Adams, Mary Baron, Michael Bérubé, Elea Carey, Cristina Case, Jim Cassidy, Terry Castle, Ilene Chazan, Miriam Chirico, Lennard Davis, Helen Deutsch, Elizabeth Donaldson, Hollie Donaldson, Christine Cipperly Dunden, George Estreich, Sandra Gilbert, Monica Gold, Molly Hand, Nina Handler, Pam Hansen, Maureen Harkin, Orin Heidelberg, Kayla Hilliar, Sujata Inyengar, Marjorie Khosrovi, Tim Ledwith, Leza Lowitz, Andrea Lunsford, Sally Coghlan McDonald, Elizabeth McKenzie, Emily Michael, Carolyn Kresse Murray, Betsy Nies, Mike Northen, Mark Osteen, Karen Poremski, Julia Miele Rodas, Ralph James Savarese, Carol Schilling, Christy Shake, Joan Venticinque, Beverly Voloshin, Kate Washington, Jillian Weise, Mike Wiley, and Mark Woods. My sincere apologies to anyone I have left out.

I also want to thank those who helped Ilene and me during our journey with August: Cindy Baccash-Pickett, Karen Barakat, Monica Beltrami, Cindy Berry, Jamie Bérubé, Judi

Bloom and Stanley Bloom, Zim Boulos and the people at OE&S, Pete Brewer, Amy Buggle and the people of DLC Nurse & Learn, Cristina and Jesse Case, Mark Cashen and the people of the Mt. Herman Exceptional Student Center, Bobby Cherry, Crawford and Helen Cole, Eric Conger, Tomi and Jack Corbett, Bradin Cormack, Angie Cosper, Eileen Davis, Scott B. Dowman, Lanier Drew, Greg and Marybeth Dyer, Susan Estilaei, Lisa Federico, Donna Ferriero, Hazel and Cathy Fong, Carlos and Nancy Frias, Rosemarie Garland-Thomson, Brian and Karen Giddens, Shannon Goossen and Arnold Graham-Smith, Mims and Dan Grifo, Pam Hansen, Kim Harris, Carolyn Hawthorne, Joe and Suzanne Honeycutt, Adrien and Patricia Jones, Annette Keogh, Barbara Lanahan, Julie Larsen, Stephen Lazoff, Betty Lituanio, Maryjane Malone, Lisa McKenzie, Sean and Lisa McNeil, Kathy Michael, Alan Mishael, Mary Fisher Orzoff, Lynn Peterson, Carlos Perera, Susan Prattos, Mark Pyatt, Carol Reaves, Kim Rickey, Linda and Wes Rieger, Chip Riegler, Ashton Taylor Roberts, Diane Silk, Piper and Cliff Spohr, Ian Stake, Niki Stokes and the Studio K moms, David Strauss, Matt Take, Jeannie Theriault, Jennifer Walsh Thomason, Chris and Lauren Trad, Steve Woodhams, and Pattye Tobase Zimmerman. I have not named everyone who helped us—that would be impossible. All of you are in our hearts.

Special thanks to all of August's caregivers throughout his fourteen years: Jamie Bérubé, Amber Boetel, Sarah Cortez, Meredith (Stoker) Frichtenicht, Kathryn "Kat" Grifo, Amanda (Vinson) Grubbs, Katrina Johnson, Christina Niccolaides, Rory Niccolaides, Jenna (Lee) Price, Jobeth (Lee) Rodrigues, Ashley (Koerick) Sauer, Skylar, Tara

(Montavani) Stamm, Stevie Coburn Thomas, and Jenna (Strongin) Troops. I am sorry if I have left anyone out. You made what seemed impossible possible.

I wish to thank my literary agent, Gillian MacKenzie, who suggested back in 2010 that I write this book, and my editor at Beacon Press, Joanna Green, who spotted possibilities in the manuscript that I didn't see. Her thoughtfulness, attention to detail, and commitment to the project brought it to fruition. Lastly, the copyeditors Chris Dodge and Susan Lumenello did a wonderful job with the manuscript.

Clio should be recognized here. She didn't ask to be the sibling of a catastrophically impaired brother, but she accepted her role with grace and flair. She was a good sister. And the love of my life Ilene should be acknowledged here too. When people marry, they rarely know what they are going to get in their partner until the chips are down. I found in Ilene the best partner there could be. She demonstrated degrees of good cheer, perseverance, fortitude, resourcefulness, and affection far beyond my ability to imagine.

Lastly, I would like to acknowledge my parents, both deceased. I miss them dearly: Frances Silvey and Arvil William Gabbard.